Fishing Knots

Fishing Knots

Proven to Work for
Light Tackle and Fly Fishing

Lefty Kreh

Illustrations by Dave Hall

SWAN·HILL
PRESS

Cover photograph by Jay Nichols
Cover design by Caroline M. Stover

Copyright © 2007 Lefty Kreh

First published in the UK in 2007
by Swan Hill Press, an imprint of Quiller Publishing Ltd

Simultaneously published in the USA by Stackpole Books

British Library Cataloguing-in-Publication Data
A catalogue record for this book
is available from the British Library

ISBN 978 1 84689 017 8

Swan Hill Press
An imprint of Quiller Publishing Ltd
Wykey House, Wykey, Shrewsbury, SY4 1JA
Tel: 01939 261616 Fax: 01939 261606
E-mail: info@quillerbooks.com
Website: www.countrybooksdirect.com

Contents

Introduction

The knot is a very important part of the fisherman's rig. No matter how superb the rod, reel, and tackle, if the knot fails the game is over. Talk to light tackle and fly fishermen about the biggest fish they've hooked and lost, and most of the time the fish escaped because the knot failed. Anglers will fuss over rods, reels, lines, lures, or flies, but ignore that most important link—the knot.

It isn't necessary to know a great many knots, but it is important to know the few knots that will do the job. Instead of including hundreds of knots in this book, I have selected the knots that will work best in any light tackle or fly-fishing situation. I have been studying knots since the 1950s, and the ones I've chosen for this book are the knots I've fished, tested, and favored over the years.

Some things are true of all knots. *No knot breaks until it slips.* To build a knot that won't slip, close the knot as firmly as possible. Sometimes a poorly designed knot that is firmly closed is stronger than a well-designed knot that is not firmly closed.

Here is a simple experiment that shows the importance of closing the knot as tightly as possible. Tie a Surgeon's Knot with a strand of 15- and 12-pound-test monofilament. (If you don't know how to tie a Surgeon's Knot, instructions are found on page 31.) Pull only on the two longer strands to close. Grasp the two long strands, one in each hand, and jerk. The knot will easily break. Make another Surgeon's Knot. But this time, pull firmly on the two longer strands and then on the two shorter ones. It makes no difference which lines you pull on first to tighten—just as long as you pull on all four strands. Now try to break the knot and you will see it is much stronger. In testing line, I have determined that you can lose as much as 40 percent of the strength of the Surgeon's Knot if you tighten only the two longer strands, allowing the shorter ones to slip. The same applies to all knots; close them as firmly as possible.

I think it is misleading to list the strength of a knot. When I am teaching students to tie knots, I have them all tie the same knot from the same line on the same type hook. Then when we test each knot, the strength of the knots may vary by as much as 30 percent. The lesson here is that some students close the knots firmly and others don't. Sure, some knots have greater potential strength if they are tied correctly. And that potential strength is what can be suggested.

Don't try to tie a new knot while you're on the water. Practice knot tying at home. Most new knots require little tricks—how to hold the line, how to make certain motions with the fingers. When you're learning a new knot, your hands will seem clumsy, but with a little practice you'll soon get the hang of it.

LINES

When it comes to lines, today's fishermen are lucky; they have many options. Decades ago, we had to choose between silk and nylon monofilament lines. Old timers will remember those silk casting lines and having to remove and dry them each night so they wouldn't rot. Then in the 1940s, Dupont invented nylon lines, which were transparent and didn't rot. But they were stiff, wiry, and the early stuff caused lots of casting problems.

Now polymers have helped to improve nylon lines. Just like when you're baking a cake, you might start with a few basic ingredients—flour, sugar, and butter—but if you add cinnamon, chocolate, some nuts, coconut, and vanilla, you change the cake slightly and make it more appealing. Polymers do the same for fishing lines. One polymer may make the line more resistant to abrasion, another makes it limper, and another gives added strength. Each manufacturer blends into a line a combination of polymers—such lines are referred to as copolymers. And they're much improved over the original Dupont formula.

When fluorocarbon lines first appeared on the market, fishermen didn't like them. We had used nylon fishing line for years and were familiar with its characteristics. Though fluorocarbon lines are similar in appearance to nylon, they behave differently. Fluorocarbon is less visible under water and sinks slightly faster. Nylon loses a little strength after it's immersed; fluorocarbon does not. Fluorocarbon is more expensive and is more difficult to knot. Nylon disintegrates when it's left outside, while fluorocarbon takes years to do so.

Manufacturers continue to experiment with polymers and other synthetics so that today's lines keep getting better. They are currently researching the effects of gamma radiation on fishing lines. Some studies seem to have shown that nylon and fluorocarbon lines subjected to gamma rays are stronger and limper because the molecular structure of the material is realigned.

Hybrid lines are also making their appearance on the market. A mix of nylon and fluorocarbon, they offer the advantages and slight disadvantages of both materials. I think they will become more popular.

Braided lines are usually made from gel-spun polyethylene material and are considerably thinner than nylon and fluorocarbon lines. DSM Performance Fibres, the Netherlands company that invented gel-spun lines, has licensed them to other manufacturers. Some manufacturers do not make their gel-spun stock material but buy it and then add their own special treatments. Adding wax, silicone, Teflon, and other materials to the line makes it smoother, more resistant to wear, and easier to cast. Take extra care when making knots in braided gel-spun lines so that knots are tight and don't slip and fail. During testing of braided gel-spun line, I have watched the line end slither through the knot and come loose as tension increases on the knots, and I am reminded of a snake threading through the branches of a tree.

The famous Bimini Twist will rarely break if properly tied in monofilament or fluorocarbon. But that is not true when the Bimini is tied with braided material. Two things to watch for when tying a Bimini with braided line: knots tied with gel-spun line tend to slip; and braided gel-spun line does not do as well in tight coils as monofilament and fluorocarbon. While some fishermen feel they need only a minimal number of twists to build a good Bimini, experienced anglers favor a 50- to 70-turn Bimini for battling strong fish. Anything less than that and they fear the Bimini will fail.

Max Garth, a pioneering Australian fly fisherman and scientist, has found a solution for gaining near or full line strength with braided gel-spun lines. Max researched the problem and in his experiments found that a knot in braided line can hold as strong as the rest of the line if you place a drop of Loctite 406 on the knot and work it in with a needle. Loctite 406 is as thin as water, and when a drop is applied and pushed into the knot, it fills the air space between the turns and locks them in place. If you can't find this glue locally, try the Internet. Go to Google, type in Loctite 406, and you'll find places to order.

Under tension, braided lines will stretch about 5 percent, whereas monofilament and fluorocarbon can stretch a good deal more. The angler fishing monofilament must learn to set the hook differently than with braided lines. Remember, it is a jerk on the line that usually breaks a knot. When a hook is set in monofilament, the line will absorb some of the shock that occurs if the hook is set hard. But because braided lines don't stretch as much, a sharp jerk on the line can cause the knot to fail. With braided line, set the hook more gently.

Braided gel-spun lines offer several advantages over other lines. For the same line strength, they are thinner than monofilament and fluorocarbon, which makes them less resistant in the water so lures can be fished deeper. Since braided gel-spun is so much stronger than monofilament and fluoro-carbon, you can use lighter lines for casting and wrestling fish from struc-ture. Anglers say that when they are using braided gel-spun lines, they are more apt to feel the light taps of a fish mouthing the lure or bait.

Conventional braided lines work well if you are jigging for largemouth or smallmouth bass or stripers in deep water. Deep jigging in salt water means dropping a lure to the bottom of a reef and then pumping it upward. With monofilament you can use this technique in depths to 200 feet. The current will sweep the larger diameter of the monofilament line sideways and impede the lure as it drops. Even worse, when you tilt the rod upward to retrieve the lure, the monofilament will stretch and the lure won't move. If you use braided line, its thinner diameter lets the lure plunge faster and deeper (you can deep jig in 400 feet of water with the right lures) and the current has fewer side effects on the lure's drop. Because there is less stretch, the lure can be more active on the retrieve, and you can be more aware of fish taking the lure. Hook setting is better.

Because Dacron is larger in diameter than gel-spun line, when lots of Dacron is pulled through the water, the drag can break the tippet. Braided gel-spun, being thinner and stronger, has less drag and is more apt to hold. Because the braided gel-spun lines are so thin, when you are installing them on a reel spool of any kind, use wet gloves to apply maximum pres-sure. Anglers using casting reels to fight a strong fish find that if the line is not installed under pressure, the entire spool of line turns on the shaft— making it impossible to retrieve line under pressure. When fly fishermen fight big fish, they have discovered that if the line is not installed under pressure the line digs into the bed of the line on the spool. Should the fish make a run, the line gets trapped among the coils and breaks.

Braided lines are expensive because the individual filaments have to be "braided," a slow and expensive process. Another type of line made from gel-spun called fusion, a twisted braid that is fused together, is less expensive but lacks many of the desirable characteristics of true braided lines.

Some knots that work well in nylon monofilament are poor performers in fluorocarbon and braided lines. Wise fishermen develop knots that match the material they use. Hook size also needs to be taken into consideration. A Clinch Knot or an Improved Clinch Knot, which works with monofilament or fluorocarbon in smaller diameters, will often unravel under stress when tied on large diameter hooks.

You'll get a poor knot if you try to connect monofilament or fluorocarbon line of a thin diameter to one with a diameter many times larger. For example, if you use a Surgeon's Knot to tie 10-pound-test to 50-pound-test, the knot will easily unravel. But when joining 10-pound-test to 20-pound-test or 30-pound-test to 50-pound-test, the Surgeon's Knot works fine. It is also more difficult to connect two strands of monofilament of different degrees of stiffness. When building a tapered fly leader, construct it all with the same brand of mono.

Lubricating monofilament and fluorocarbon helps get tighter knots, but fluorocarbon is a bit slippery and too much lube can make closing the knot difficult. With fluorocarbon it is best to lubricate with water and not saliva, since saliva often contains a bit of oil, which doesn't help close the knot properly.

Monofilament can be damaged. Anglers sometimes wonder how long they can store mono before it begins to deteriorate. If you have a number of spools in storage, mark each spool with the date of purchase and use the oldest first. Store monofilament away from sunlight and fluorescent lights and in a normal room temperature (not too dry), and it should last for years. Since trout tippets are fragile, replace them every two years. Anytime the line seems to change color or a whitish dust appears on the line, discard it. Fluorocarbon does not deteriorate, so fragile trout tippet material need not be discarded every two or three years. An advantage of gel-spun braids is that they are not harmed by sunlight, aging, oil, and other materials that affect nylon.

LEADERS

A leader is the part of a line that is connected to a lure, bait, or fly. It can be a single strand or a number of strands. If you are fishing for sharp-toothed fish, the end of the leader should have wire connected to the lure, bait, or fly, but the rest of the leader can be of another material.

A fly-fishing leader may be tapered. The largest diameter of a tapered leader is called the butt section; the next portion is called the midsection; and the section with the smallest and weakest diameter that attaches to a fly is called the tippet, or class tippet.

Many anglers who use spinning and plug-casting outfits connect a single, heavy strand of monofilament or fluorocarbon to the line on the reel. The thinner line on the reel allows them to make longer casts with less effort, and the heavier length of line between the light line and the lure or bait prevents a hooked fish from cutting or abrading the line during a fight. For my favorite freshwater fish, the smallmouth bass, which is often found on rocky bottoms, I use 6- or 8-pound-test spinning line to cast my lures and attach a 10-foot section of 10-pound-test between the lighter line and the lure.

Sometimes a heavier section, called a shock or bite tippet, is attached to the tippet as well. Shock leaders were developed for surf fishermen, who use long rods to cast heavy baits or lures considerable distances from shore. In surf casting, so much stress is put on the fragile casting line that the weight of the bait or lure can snap the line. A stronger line attached to the bait or lure and long enough to wrap several times around the reel spool permits the angler to use the force required on long casts. This heavier length of line is aptly called a shock leader.

Some fly fishermen have also used the term "shock leader" to describe a short length of heavier line on the end of a fragile tippet. When tarpon fishing (because that fish has an abrasive mouth), they may attach a 60- to 100-pound short length of monofilament or fluorocarbon between the tippet and the fly. "Shock leader" is not a good term for this rig because little shock occurs. Better to call it a bite leader, since it prevents the fish from wearing or biting through the leader portion attached to the fly. I use both names to prevent confusion.

There are two kinds of leaders. One allows the angler to manipulate the bait, lure, or fly. The other is designed to do the exact opposite and not affect the natural drifting motion of the fly in the current. Fly fishermen fishing for cold-water species such as steelhead and trout use tapered leaders of the latter style.

Anglers seeking world records should use special knots developed for connecting diameters of lines of different weights and materials. This book lists what I consider the essential knots to accomplish these tasks.

Tapered Fly-Fishing Leaders

Fly fishermen can frighten wary fish in clear, shallow water if they let their line splash down on the surface. Using a tapered leader can solve this problem. The rear butt section of a tapered leader is heavier than the tippet end, allowing most of the energy from the cast to dissipate before the tippet falls to the surface.

There are many tapered leader designs. To better understand their design we need to look at the fly line. A fly line is not cast; instead it is *unrolled* to the target. What allows the line to completely unroll is the caster imparting enough energy so that the fly line's flexible weight can reach the target.

The same principle is true for a tapered leader. Fly-fishing myths are many, and one of them is that the butt section should be a stiff nylon. Stiff nylon does not want to unroll like a fly line. The butt section should be a flexible weight and long enough so the leader continues to unroll.

A properly designed tapered leader needs enough flexible weight in the butt section to transfer energy from the line to the leader. The butt section should be half the length of a tapered leader—and heavy enough. The best material to build your tapered leader with is a premium spinning line. These high quality lines are strong enough to support good knots, are consistent in their diameter, and are limp. To maintain uniformity, use the same manufacturer's material throughout.

Here is an example of how to build a good 9- to 10-foot tapered leader for an 8- or 9-weight fly line fly. Use 5 feet of 50-pound-test, one foot of 40-pound-test, one foot of 30-pound-test, one foot of 20-pound-test, and 18 to 24 inches of 15-, 12-, or 10-pound-test tippet. For most tapered leaders (except those used for dry-fly fishing), I prefer tippets 18 to 24 inches long. Longer tippets tend to gather leader-weakening knots.

If you want a 12-foot tapered leader (often used for bonefish), the butt section should be 6 feet long and then tapered down to the tippet. When fishing conditions are very calm, I often use a 16-foot leader for wary bonefish and carp in low clear water. With an 8-foot length of flexible heavy butt leader, it is amazing how well the leader turns over—even if there is a breeze.

I have not used diameters to indicate the butt sections since few fishermen carry micrometers. Pound test is close enough for practical purposes. It is important to understand that if you are a few inches off in any one of the tapered sections, it's no problem as long as the butt section is the correct pound test and half the length of the tapered leader. I have had great success using the following diameters with these lines: for 6- and 7-weight fly lines, a butt section of 40 pounds; for 8- and 9-weight lines, a butt section of 50 pounds; for 10- through 12-weight lines, 60 pounds.

I no longer make my own dry-fly leaders. I prefer to buy commercial ones with supple butt sections half the length of the leader. I use a simple technique to extend the life of dry-fly leaders. The tippet of almost all manufactured leaders is no more than 24 inches long. After you've fished a number of flies—tied them on and cut them off—you'll have used that 24 inches of tippet. If you attach another tippet, then a portion of the leader is used each time. Soon that nicely tapered leader is no longer tapered. When I buy a new leader, I cut the first 24 inches from it—the entire tippet. I then make a Kreh Loop in the clipped end. You can also use a Six-Turn Surgeon's Loop, but I prefer to tie a Kreh Loop because I find it stronger. When the tippet is tied in with a Kreh Loop and it gets too short, I can simply un-loop and discard it, tie on another, and the leader will last many trips. If the loop on the main leader gets worn, retie another. So little material is used that it doesn't affect performance.

Glossary

leader: A length of line that connects a hook, fly, or lure to the main fishing line.

line: Throughout this text, the word "line" is used in a general sense to describe everything from rope to tippet to leader material.

loop: A closed U-shaped section of line.

main line (standing part of the line): The inactive section of line between the tag end and reel connection (or the longer end of the line, if you're working with leader material).

tag end: The part of the line in which the knot is tied. Also refers to the short piece of line that remains after a knot is tied, which is usually trimmed.

turn or wrap: A complete revolution of one line around another that is often formed by passing the tag end around the standing part of the line.

The tying instructions provided in this book are for right-handers.

1

Basic Knots

There are many knots, each with a purpose. Nearly all knots are a form of Nail, Overhand, or Clinch Knot—or a combination of these.

Illustrated here are the three basic knots: the Overhand, the Clinch, and the Nail Knot.

THE OVERHAND KNOT

The Overhand Knot is a weak connection on its own. But I have included it here because it is an important step in several stronger and more complicated knots.

Step 1: With the thumb and forefinger of your left hand, hold the standing part of the line about eight inches from the tag end. Hold the tag end between the thumb and forefinger of your right hand. Form a simple loop in the line by rotating your right hand and bringing it toward your left.

Pinch the loop together with your left hand, and with your right hand pass the tag end over the standing part of the line and through the loop.

Step 2: Moisten the knot and pull both hands steadily apart to tighten.

IMPROVED CLINCH KNOT

This is perhaps the most popular knot for attaching monofilament or fluorocarbon lines to a swivel, hook, fly, or lure. Yet it is not as strong as a number of other knots and is a poor knot in braided or Dacron line. Some other knots—such as the Orvis (or Becker) and Fisherman's Knot— are easier to tie and superior in strength, and I suggest investigating them. The Improved Clinch Knot is also difficult to properly close by hand with lines testing more than 20 pounds.

Step 1: Insert enough of the tag end (about 3 to 5 inches) through the eye of the hook or swivel to build the knot. Make five complete turns with the tag end around the main line.

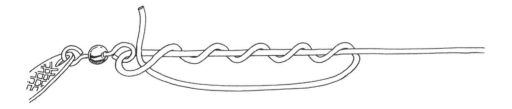

Step 2: Insert the tag end through the small loop in front of the eye.

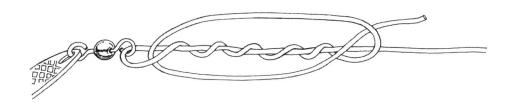

Step 3: Then bring the tag end through the larger line loop. Pull gently on the tag end until the larger loop lies against the smaller coils in the line.

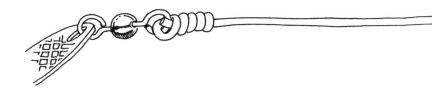

Step 4: Wet the knot and pull on both the tag end and the main line to close the knot. Make sure none of the turns overlap each other; this will weaken the knot.

Trim the tag end.

TUBE NAIL KNOT

A Nail Knot is very versatile. You can use it to attach the leader to the fly line and the fly line to the backing. To tie a Tube Nail Knot, use a hollow tube. It is best to use the smallest tube possible, since the loose coils need to be tightened after the tube is extracted. The smaller the tube, the smaller the coils and the easier the process will be.

The advantage of using a tube to build the Nail Knot is that it can be placed anywhere on a fishing line. There are several reasons for doing this. For example, if you are fly-fishing at night, you may not know when you have retrieved enough line to make an easy backcast. If you don't retrieve enough line, it will be difficult to make the backcast. If you retrieve too much line, you'll end up having to make extra false casts. If you install a Nail Knot on the line at the proper location, you can feel the knot and retrieve just the right amount of line to make the backcast.

This technique also works for a novice caster who is learning how much line to retrieve for making good backcasts. There are times, especially when night fishing the surf, where the fly must be retrieved almost to the leader. By placing a second Nail Knot on the line so that you don't retrieve the leader into the guides, you'll know when to stop retrieving and begin another cast.

These drawings show a Tube Nail Knot used to attach a leader to a fly line.

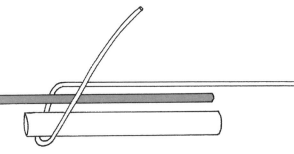

Step 1: Position the end of the fly line even with one end of the tube. Lay the leader along the fly line and then make one wrap around the fly line and tube with the tag end of the leader.

Step 2: Begin winding the tag end of the leader toward the end of the fly line. Make five to seven turns. The closer together you make the coils the easier the knot will close. Use your thumb and finger to keep the coils together.

From this point on, it is important to keep tension on the tag end of the leader, or the coils will unravel.

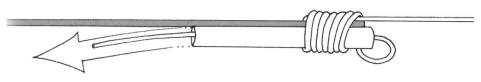

Step 3: Once the coils have been formed, pull on the tag end of the leader to draw the coils together. Then insert the tag end of the leader through the tube while holding the coils together. Remove the tube from under the coils.

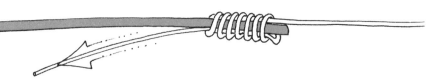

Step 4: Carefully tease all coils so they lie snugly against each other. To tighten firmly, be sure to pull on both strands of the leader, forming the Nail Knot.

Step 5: Trim the tag ends.

TIP

Connecting the butt section to a fly line with a Nail Knot leaves a bump that can catch in the rod guides. To smooth out the connection, coat the knot with Pliobond or a similar flexible glue to form a football shape.

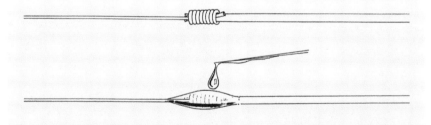

2

Connecting Lines

BLOOD KNOT

The Blood Knot (often called the Barrel Knot) is a popular method of joining dissimilar strands of monofilament or fluorocarbon lines. It is most frequently used to build tapered leaders for fly fishing. The Blood Knot consists of two Clinch Knots. It is not recommended for braided gel-spun lines.

Step 1: Place the main lines side-by-side with the tag ends opposite each other and make a series of wraps with one tag end around the other line. With line testing more than 25 pounds, only three turns are recommended. Increase the number of turns as the line diameter decreases. For example, with lines testing less than 8 pounds, make six turns with the smaller line.

At this point, you can eliminate a problem that might occur when forming the rest of the knot. As shown in the illustration for step 1, form a loop with the active main line in front of the first turn and pinch it with your thumb and finger to hold it in position. After making the required twists around the line, insert the active tag end up through the loop between the active main line and the second tag end.

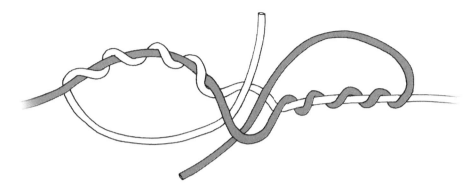

Step 2: Continue to hold the loop with your thumb and finger. Now take the second tag end and make the required number of turns around the other main line as shown. Then insert the second tag end down through the loop between the two lines. Carefully hold the loosely formed connections with both hands and place them between your lips. Gently pull on both main lines, allowing the twist to form the knot.

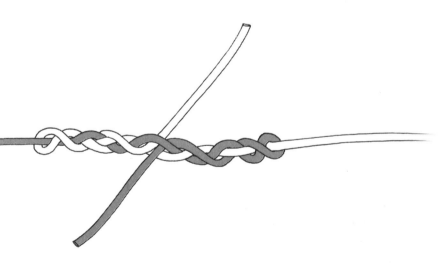

Step 3: Remember that any Clinch Knot can be difficult to close properly unless all strands lie against the spirals. This is accomplished by gently pulling on each tag end until the formed knot looks like the illustration for step 3.

Step 4: Lubricate the knot and slowly but firmly pull on the two main lines to seat the knot correctly. Trim the tag ends flush.

TIP

A nick in monofilament drastically reduces the line's strength. After landing a fish or whenever you suspect the line has been nicked, you should check the line. A quick way to do this is to place the monofilament between your first finger and thumb. Push down on the monofilament until your thumbnail is depressed into your finger. Continue to press the mono tight against your finger and pull the line; if there is a nick, you will feel it. It is always a good idea after landing a big fish to cut the leader close to the fly and discard any that's been in contact with the fish and retie.

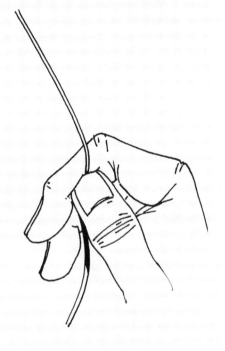

ALBRIGHT KNOT

Fishermen frequently need to join one line to another of larger diameter or to connect solid braided wire to a fishing line. The Albright Knot has served this purpose well for more than fifty years. It is not only a serviceable knot but is also an attractive one when completed. While it performs fairly well with braided gel-spun lines, there are better knots, such as the Huffnagle Knot, for this purpose.

When connecting one line to another with a larger diameter, it is best to make a Bimini Twist (see page 36 for instructions) in the lighter line before building the knot if maximum strength is desired. If connecting solid wire to a fishing line, it is best to construct a Haywire Twist (see page 70 for instructions) in the wire and then flatten the wire loop before making an Albright. Otherwise, the wire under pressure will sometimes slither through the Albright, allowing the fish to escape.

Step 1: Form a horseshoe shape in the larger line to be attached to the line from the reel. (If solid wire is used, make a Haywire Twist loop instead of the horseshoe shape.) Insert the tag end of the line inside the horseshoe shape or wire loop as shown.

Step 2: Squeeze the horseshoe shape together and, working left to right, make at least twelve turns with the tag end of the line around the two strands of the heavier line or wire loop. Be careful not to overlap any of the strands. If an overlap occurs, the line will sometimes break. After the wraps are made, insert the tag end through the U of the horseshoe-shaped heavier line or wire loop as shown. Note: Both ends of the line should now be on the same side of the U in the heavier line.

Step 3: Tease the coils close to the end of the U. Be careful not to slide them over the end. When closing the knot, it is important to pull firmly on the tag end of the line first. This prevents the coils from unraveling off the heavier line. Then pull on the main line so that all the coils are brought snugly together. Finally, pull on the tag end again to make sure the knot is closed as tightly as possible.

Step 4: To lock the knot so it won't come loose, make six half hitches around the main line with the tag end. Tease the half hitches down until they are firmly closed against the Albright. This will lock the knot securely.

Step 5: Clip the two tag ends close to the knot.

TIP

Once a knot has been securely closed, any protruding ends should be clipped flush. Dangling ends can tangle a leader tippet. On smaller flies, dangling tag ends spoil the appearance and performance of the fly on the retrieve.

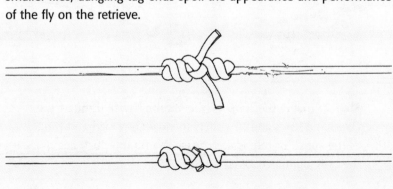

HUFFNAGLE KNOT

There are a number of situations where the angler wants the strongest connection to connect a thinner line to a thicker or stronger line. For this purpose, the Huffnagle works well. Begin by making a Bimini Twist in the lighter line. When tied correctly, the Bimini is near main line strength and forms a straight connection between the thinner and heavier line, allowing lures and flies to track properly on the retrieve.

The Huffnagle Knot is smaller than almost any other similar connection. In world-record fly fishing, all knots are considered a part of the shock or bite leader. The smaller the knot, the more shock or bite leader can be used. The Huffnagle Knot allows you to use the full length of the shock or bite leader. The Huffnagle is designed for either monofilament or fluorocarbon and is not recommended for braided gel-spun lines.

Step 1: Make an Overhand Knot in the shock or bite leader. Do not close the knot.

Step 2: Insert the loop of the Bimini Twist through the Overhand Knot and use pliers to close the Overhand Knot in the shock or bite leader. Tease the Bimini flush against the now-tightened Overhand Knot.

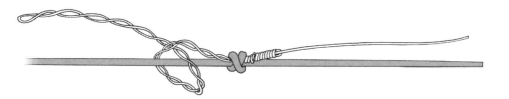

Step 3: Use the Bimini Twist loop to make an Overhand Knot around the shock or bite leader. Tease it gently and close it tightly against the Overhand Knot.

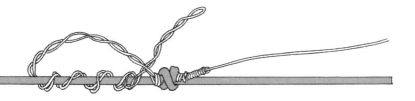

Step 4: Working left to right, use the loop end to make five half hitches around the shock or bite leader.

Step 5: Pull on the loop end to firmly close it against the Overhand Knot.

Step 6: Trim the tag ends.

SLIM BEAUTY

The Slim Beauty is a rather new knot that has gained acceptance by anglers around the world. It is one of the best knots to attach a fluoro-carbon or monofilament line to a similar heavier or stronger shock or bite leader.

The Slim Beauty is a quick and easy knot to tie. Tying a Slim Beauty with a single strand of mono (not employing a Bimini Twist) to a heavier bite or shock leader produces a very small knot. This knot is especially effective when you use casting plug or spinning tackle where the main line is less than 15-pound-test and you want to use a longer and slightly heavier length to connect to this line and then to a lure or bait. When fishing for smallmouth bass, I prefer 6- or 8-pound-test on the reel—but many times I'll add two or three yards of 10-pound-test mono as a long shock or bite leader.

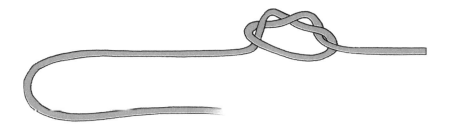

Step 1: Make a Double Overhand Knot in the heavier line (shock or bite leader).

Step 2: Slowly pull on the two ends until the knot resembles a Figure-8.

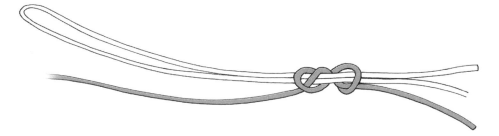

Step 3: Double the thinner strand so that it forms a loop about 18 inches long. Insert the single strand loop straight through both loops of the Figure-8 as shown. After wetting the knot, close the Figure-8 Knot firmly with pliers.

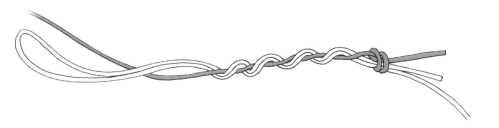

Step 4: Make four wraps with the doubled lighter line around the heavier shock or bite leader. The number of wraps is a personal choice. Some anglers believe four wraps are enough and others think six to ten wraps are better.

Step 5: Then wrap the loop back over the first wraps three times toward the Figure-8.

Step 6: Insert the end of the loop through the gap formed between the Figure-8 Knot and the first wrap made. Wet the wraps around the shock or bite leader or you may have trouble closing the knot. Do not pull on the end of the doubled loop to tighten the knot. Grasp the heavier line firmly (gripping it with pliers often helps) and begin pulling on the single strand (main line). This will slowly cause the wraps to form like a Blood Knot as they are compressed toward the Figure-8 Knot. Make sure no coils overlap.

Step 7: Once all wraps are against the Figure-8, firmly close the Figure-8 and then pull as hard as possible on the main line to complete the connection. Trim the ends of the loop and the tag end of the heavier shock or bite leader.

SURGEON'S KNOT

This is one of the quickest and easiest knots for joining dissimilar diameters of fluorocarbon or monofilament lines. It can be used to attach a tippet to the end of a tapered leader. With the Surgeon's Knot, you can tie plastic-coated braided wire testing less than 60 pounds to monofilament or fluorocarbon. The Surgeon's Knot is not recommended with braided gelspun or Dacron lines. The Surgeon's Knot is a good one to use when you're fly-fishing for trout and it's getting dark and you need to connect a slender tippet to your leader. With practice, you'll be able to tie a Surgeon's Knot behind your back.

It is difficult to close a Surgeon's Knot tight enough in lines testing more than 40 pounds. To join monofilament or fluorocarbon lines testing 6 pounds or less, pass the tag ends through the circle of line four times (Double Surgeon's Knot).

Step 1: To start, place the two tag ends opposing each other.

Step 2: Wrap the tag ends loosely around your first two fingers. Remove the circle from around your two fingers and pass the two tag ends through the circle, forming an Overhand Knot.

Step 3: Take the two tag ends through the circle again, forming a Double Overhand Knot.

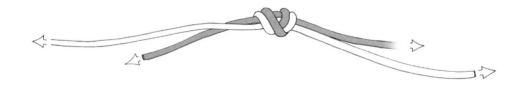

Step 4: Wet the knot and carefully draw the knot closed. Very important: To obtain maximum knot strength, you must pull on both tag ends and both long ends. The order doesn't matter, but you must pull firmly on all four strands. If you don't, you could end up with a knot that is half as strong as it could be. When closing the Surgeon's Knot, it should resemble a Figure-8. If it doesn't, tease the strands so it does. If the knot does not resemble a Figure-8 when finally closed, it will be weak and will probably fail.

Trim the tag ends flush.

How to Make a Faster Knot

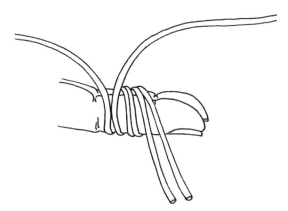

Step 1: To build a faster Surgeon's Knot, begin by making two wraps with the tag ends around your finger.

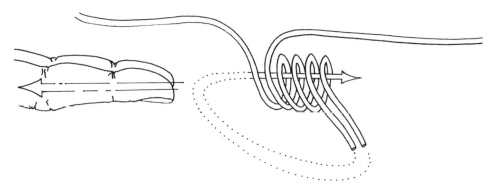

Step 2: Slip the wraps from your finger and pass the two tag ends through the wraps once and close the knot.

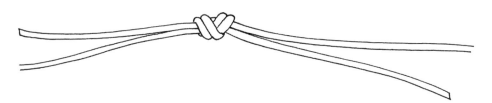

Step 3: You'll end up with a Surgeon's Knot that is the same as the original, but you've eliminated a step and saved some time.

3

Knots

BIMINI TWIST

The Bimini Twist is one of the most popular knots worldwide for reinforcing line with another piece of line for maximum strength. If tied correctly, the knot doesn't slip, so the line can perform at full strength. The two legs of the loops let you tie a knot with the two strands of the Bimini, ensuring a very strong knot.

The Bimini Twist performs well in monofilament and fluorocarbon lines but is not as efficient in Dacron and modern braided gel-spun lines. The standard for many years has been to make twenty twists in the loop. That's okay in monofilament, fluorocarbon, or Dacron lines, but Bimini Twists constructed with braided gel-spun lines tend to slip under pressure if only twenty turns are made. Most experienced fishermen agree that with braided gel-spun lines, you should make fifty to sixty twists before finishing the Bimini Twist. To ensure that the Bimini Twist doesn't fail with braided lines, firmly secure the knot with a drop of Loctite 406.

When using monofilament or fluorocarbon lines, you can add twists to create a shock absorber. Building fifty to sixty twists in mono before finishing the Bimini allows the knot loop to stretch like a rubber band, a desirable trait when you're fishing very light lines where a quick jerk could break off a fighting fish.

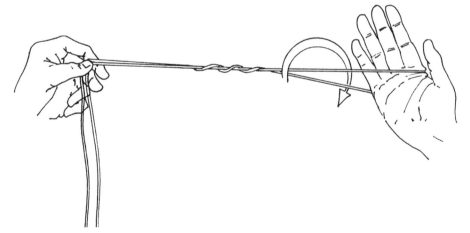

Step 1: Pull off enough line to make the desired Bimini Twist. Grasp the tag end and the main line firmly with one hand, making a loop. Slip the other hand inside the loop and make the desired number of twists.

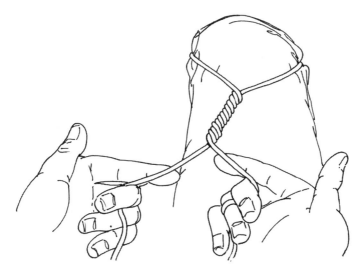

Step 2: Slide the loop over your knee, making sure the knee is bent at less than a right angle to prevent the loop from slipping off. Grasp the main line with your left hand and the tag end with your right and slowly and evenly spread them apart, which will force the twists toward the knee. Continue until the twists touch your knee. This will ensure that the finished loop will have even twists throughout.

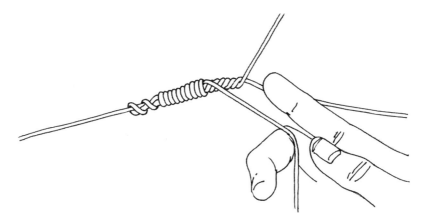

Step 3: Move your left hand to the right so the main line is now straight and in line with your body, being sure to keep both lines taut. Important: With your right hand, move the tag end so that it is at slightly more than a right

angle to the twists. Creep your right hand close to the twists, always maintaining tautness in the tag end. Slip your finger under the loop and begin pushing upward to cause the tag end to start rolling around the twists. To obtain maximum strength in the knot, it is important that the first two turns around the twists are spiraled. After that the turns should be close together.

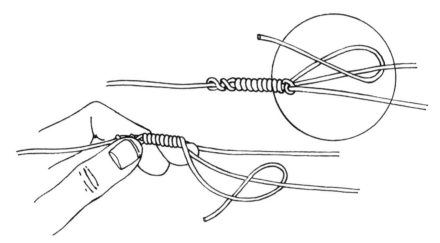

Step 4: While keeping tension on the main line, creep your left hand up so you can pinch the wraps and trap them. Now with your right hand, make a half hitch with the tag end around one leg of the loop and then another half hitch on the other leg. This is especially important with braided lines so that when the line is being strained, the two legs of the coil exert even pressure in a knot.

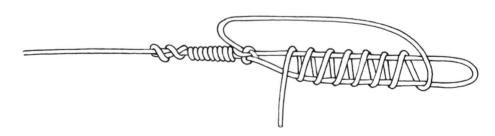

Step 5: Use the tag end to make six turns around both legs of the loop.

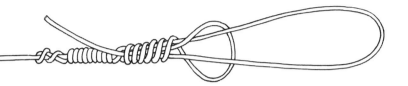

Step 6: After you have made six coils with the tag end around the two legs of the Bimini loop, place the tag end so it lies alongside the main line and is at least an inch past the Bimini. Pinch the main line, the Bimini, and the tag end in one hand, and with the other hand grasp one leg of the loop and make five turns around both legs of the Bimini loop, being sure to position each of the turns tight against the Bimini. This removes the twists created by turning the six coils around both legs of the Bimini loop that often make closing the knot difficult. The loop is now free of twists.

Step 7: Continue to pinch the Bimini and the turns around the two legs and then grasp the tag end and pull firmly on it to close the loop and the knot.

100% ARBOR KNOT

Bill Nash of San Jose, California, knows a lot about fishing knots and has developed a way of attaching the backing line to the fly reel spool that delivers 100 percent line strength.

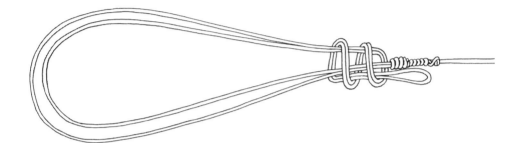

Step 1: Tie a Bimini Twist in the backing line end with a resulting loop that is at least 24 inches long. If using gel-spun line, make a 70-twist Bimini or add a drop of Loctite 406 to the Bimini to guarantee 100 percent strength. Using the doubled lines, form a loop ending with a two-turn Nail Knot. Hold the loops in one hand while tightening the Nail Knot with the other hand.

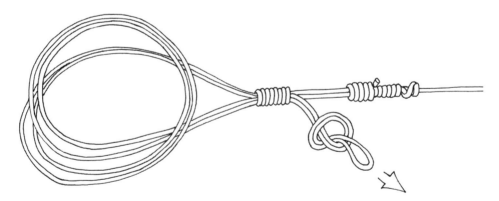

Step 2: Form an Overhand Knot in the end of the loop and tease it close to the Nail Knot before tightening. Trim the end.

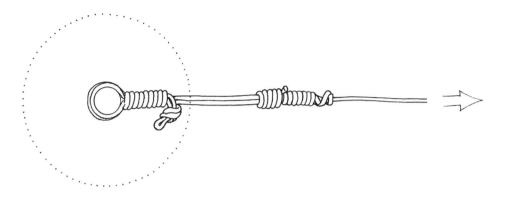

Step 3: Remove the spool from the reel and pass the double loop over the spool rim and onto the reel arbor. Pull on the main line to tighten the loops on the shaft. You may have to work the main line back and forth to close the loops completely.

TIP

100% Knot

A 100 percent knot is one that is just as strong as the line in which there is no knot. A knot that's badly tied makes the line weak. A knot that slips makes the line weak.

UNI-KNOT, OR DUNCAN LOOP

The Uni-Knot, also called the Duncan Loop, is popular and can be used to attach two dissimilar sizes of monofilament or fluorocarbon lines or to attach either of these lines to braided or solid wire. It is not recommended for braided gel-spun lines unless you add a drop of Loctite 406. This knot is one of the most versatile; anglers use it for a variety of purposes. It can be used as a loop in front of lure or fly, it's easy to tie around large objects, and a Uni-Knot-to-Uni-Knot is often used to make tapered leaders.

The Uni-Knot is also a popular method of making a loop knot. It is not as strong as a Non-Slip or Kreh Loop since it is a form of the Clinch Knot. However, you can tie it in heavier lines such as 60- to 120-pound-test monofilament to be used as a shock or bite leader. Pliers must be used to properly close knots with larger lines.

The illustration shows how to form a Uni-Knot Loop. If a loop is not desired, simply pull on the main line to firmly close it.

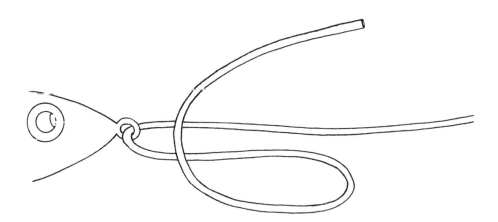

Step 1: Insert the tag end through the eye of the hook or lure. Fold the tag end back away from the eye to form a loop.

Step 2: Pass the tag end four to six times around the two lines.

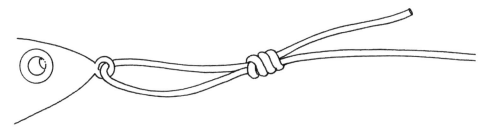

Step 3: Pull on the tag end to close all coils around the main line.

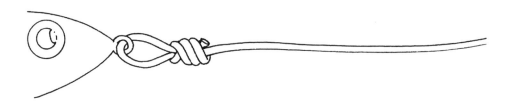

Step 4: If a loop is desired, hold the hook or lure securely and pull on the main line. This causes the coils to move toward the eye. Stop when you have the desired size loop size. If heavier monofilament line is used, make sure the hook or lure is held firmly, then pull on the tag end with pliers to complete the knot.

If no loop is desired, simply pull on the main line until the knot contacts the eye. Pull on the tag end with pliers with heavier lines to seat the knot.

Trim the tag end.

Using the Uni-Knot Loop to Join Two Lines

Step 1: To connect two lines with Uni-Knots, form one Uni-Knot loop. Then pass the tag end of the second line through this loop. Tie a Uni-Knot loop in the second line. You now have two loops connected. Make sure the coils in each line are formed close together.

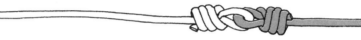

Step 2: Pull on both main lines, causing the knots to join the two lines together. Pull firmly on each tag end to seat the knot properly.

TIP

It is important to install gel-spun braided lines to your spool as firmly as possible. One good way to apply pressure is to press the line with a gloved hand when putting it on the spool.

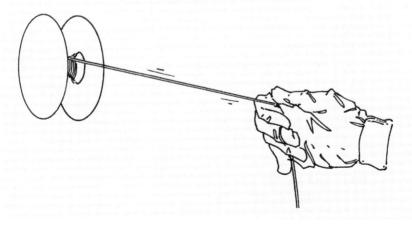

ATTACHING LINE TO THE REEL SPOOL

This is one of the most secure methods of attaching line to the reel spool. Some fly fishermen wrap the line once or twice around the spool with Dacron backing. With gel-spun lines (especially on plug casting reels), make two wraps of duct tape on the spool shaft before installing the line to prevent it from slipping under fighting pressure.

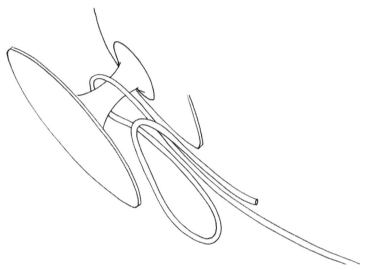

Step 1: Make one or more wraps around the spool shaft and begin the Uni-Knot (or Duncan Loop).

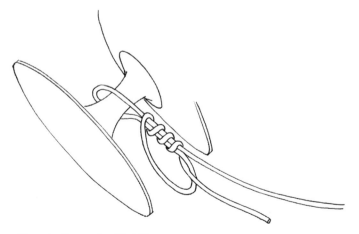

Step 2: Form the Uni-Knot.

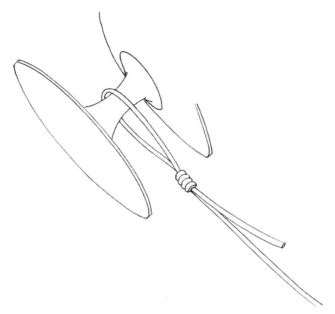

Step 3: Pull firmly on the tag end to close the Uni-Knot.

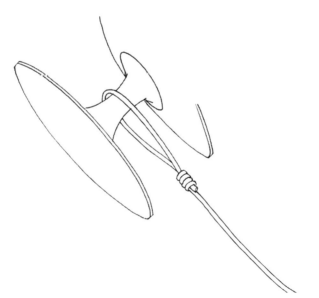

Step 4: Trim the tag end flush and pull on the main line, which will slide the knot tight against the reel shaft.

GEORGE HARVEY DRY FLY KNOT

This is my favorite way to connect a dry fly to a tippet. It looks complicated but actually is not. The knot has several advantages. It is nearly 100
percent of tippet strength when closed properly. The knot is also secured
on the fly's thread head behind the hook eye. Instead of tying the tippet to
a thin size 20 or smaller wire hook, secure the knot so the coils are cush-
ioned on the thread. Once the knot is closed correctly, the fly can never
cock or tilt on the tippet, ensuring that it floats properly on every cast. If
the knot is correctly formed, the coils won't slip over the hook eye before
the knot is closed. This knot also works well for small nymphs and
Atlantic salmon flies.

Note: This knot cannot be tied on a ring-eye hook. It must be tied on
a hook with a turned-up or turned-down eye.

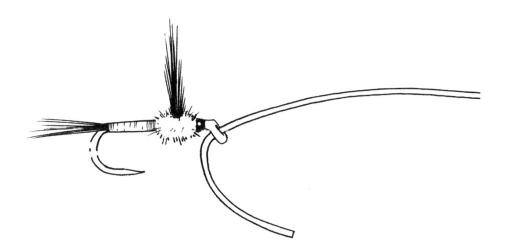

Step 1: Insert about 4 inches of the tag end through the
eye of the hook. Don't worry about using too much tippet
to form the knot. When closing the knot, slide the tippet
back through the hook eye so that only a few inches of
tippet are available to build the knot.

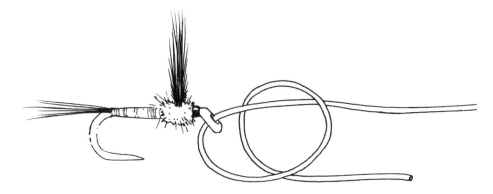

Step 2: Hold the two strands of the tippet in front of the fly. You will not hold the hook again until the knot is completely formed and closure begins. Make sure the tag end is pointing toward your body and then take the tag end over the top of the main line and form a circular coil with the tag end around the main line. Make a full circle, not a spiral.

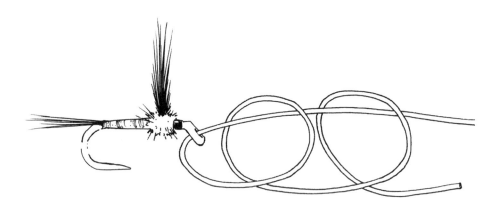

Step 3: Make another circle around the main line. Try to form the coils so they are no larger than $^3/_8$ inch in diameter.

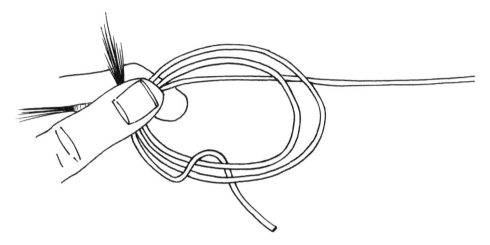

Step 4: Slide the two coils under your forefinger and thumb while clenching the main line. Now pass the tag end through the bottom of the two coils.

Important: Do not pass the tag end around the main line.

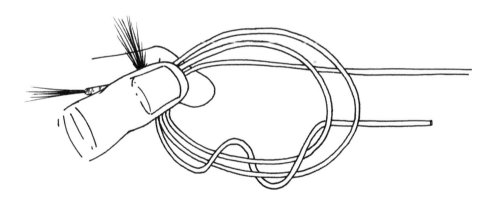

Step 5: Pass the tag end again through the bottom of the two coils while still clenching the main line and coils with your finger and thumb.

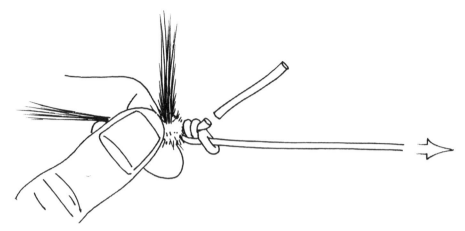

Step 6: Release the main line and coils, grasp the hook, and slowly pull on the main line. The two coils will move toward the hook eye and finally jump over it. (If the coils fail to jump over the hook eye, you've made a mistake in forming the knot.) Once you have pulled on the main line, the tag end, and the hook, the knot will close on the threads.

Trim the tag end.

TIP

Not only should you use pressure to install gel-spun braided on a reel spool, you should also crosshatch the line on the spool in small Xs to help prevent the line from burying and snapping when you are fighting a good fish.

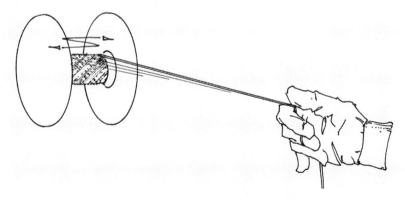

4

Lines and
Leaders

WORLD RECORD FLY LEADERS

The following four illustrations are examples of how to construct fly leaders that conform to world record rules. Each one has a 60-pound butt section, though you can choose one that's heavier or lighter. The thinnest portion is the class tippet, which has a Bimini Twist on each end that attaches the butt section and the shock or bite leader of monofilament, fluorocarbon, flexible or solid wire.

According to IFGA rules, a butt section can be of any length. However, the class tippet and its knots must be at least 15 inches long and the shock or bite leader no longer than 12 inches, including all knots between the hook eye and the class tippet.

Solid Wire to Fly Leader

Fly fishermen need to use a bite leader of wire when seeking fish with teeth. Plastic-coated and nickel-titanium braided wires have the disadvantage of being thicker in diameter than solid stainless steel trolling wire. If you use thicker wire in clear water or with sharp-eyed fish such as wahoo and tuna, the fish may refuse to strike. The disadvantage of a solid wire leader is that it kinks badly while fighting the fish.

To connect solid wire to the monofilament, do not use a standard Albright Knot. Under stress the wire will sometimes slither through the knot, and you'll lose the fish. Instead, it is best to first make a Haywire Twist to form a loop, which is flattened, and then attach the Albright to it. For more information on the Haywire Twist, see page 70.

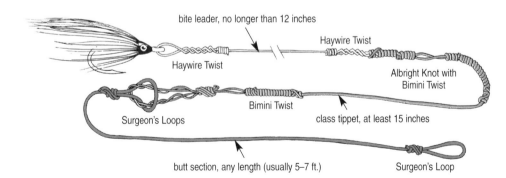

bite leader, no longer than 12 inches

Haywire Twist

Haywire Twist

Albright Knot with Bimini Twist

Surgeon's Loops

Bimini Twist

class tippet, at least 15 inches

butt section, any length (usually 5–7 ft.)

Surgeon's Loop

Nickel-Titanium Braided Wire to Fly Leader

Modern plastic-coated wire is made from many strands of nickel-titanium. It has advantages over the older plastic-coated braided wire. Nickel-titanium is more flexible, much thinner in the same strength, and is easier to tie. Manufacturers claim that monofilament knots work well with nickel-titanium braided wire. But experienced fly fishermen working on strong fish have found that a two-turn Non-Slip Loop or Kreh Loop is the best connection to the fly. It gives the fly more action and is very strong.

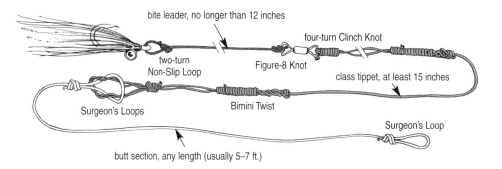

Plastic-Coated Braided Wire to Fly Leader

The easiest and quickest way to attach wire to a fly leader is with inexpensive plastic-coated wire. This wire has a fairly large diameter and is often used with fish that are not leader-shy, such as bluefish.

The simple Figure-8 Knot is the best choice for attaching this wire to hooks and swivels. Because wire has to be changed frequently when fish deform it during the fight, one of the most convenient methods of replacing the wire is to connect it to a barrel swivel attached to the monofilament leader.

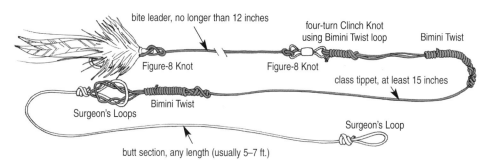

Saltwater Leader with Heavy Mono Tippet

A clear, heavy (40- to 120-pound-test) monofilament shock or bite tippet is used when fishing in clear water for many leader-shy fish that do not have sharp teeth, such as tarpon.

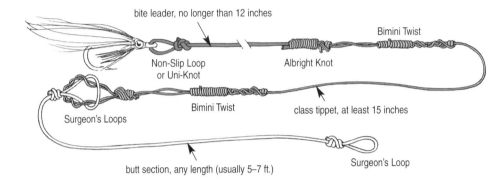

bite leader, no longer than 12 inches

Bimini Twist

Non-Slip Loop or Uni-Knot

Albright Knot

Surgeon's Loops

Bimini Twist

class tippet, at least 15 inches

butt section, any length (usually 5–7 ft.)

Surgeon's Loop

TIP

Fly fishermen on the water often have problems straightening heavy, clear mono used for bite leaders. Obtain a section of half-inch copper pipe or tubing. Cut enough lengths of the heavy monofilament to fill the tubing and place them inside. Lay the tube filled with the

80 POUND

lengths of mono in a large open pan filled with water. Place the pan on the stove and bring the water in the pan to a boil. Set it aside for a few minutes. Then with pliers, lift the tube from the hot water and douse it with cold water. The mono strands will now be straight. Store them in a section of half-inch plastic pipe, and they are ready for use.

TWO METHODS OF CONNECTING A SHOOTING LINE TO A SHOOTING HEAD

Shooting heads (also called shooting tapers) are attached to a thinner shooting line—allowing longer casts. The most common method uses a loop in the shooting head and another in the thinner shooting line. This allows you to quickly change different heads to the same shooting line. You may be using a floating shooting head and then the fishing situation might call for a sinking head. Loops permit this quick change.

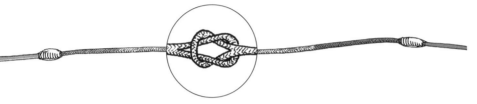

A: This setup shows how the head and shooting line are attached with loops. It is important that the loops be joined with what resembles a square knot. A girth hitch will weaken the connection. Different types of materials can be used to form the loops, but the most popular material is hollow braided line.

B: This setup demonstrates another method of connecting a shooting head to a shooting line. The head is inserted in one end of hollow braided line and the shooting line in the other end. This system forms a smooth, strong connection. The disadvantage to this method is that you can't change heads. You may prefer this setup if you object to the loops, which can catch in the fly rod guides. See page 89 to learn how to connect hollow braided line to form a loop or attach it to a fly line.

LEADER CONNECTIONS

Here are four popular ways to connect the fly line to the leader and the backing:

1. Nail Knot
2. Whipped Loop
3. Double Nail Knot Loop
4. Braided Line Loop

The Nail Knot is perhaps the oldest and most common method of connecting the leader to the line. It became popular when the famed writer Joe Brooks introduced it in the 1950s. One disadvantage of this method is that the knot forms a permanent connection, making it difficult to change leaders to suit different fishing conditions. Unless the Nail Knot is smoothly coated, it can also snag in the fly rod guides while you're landing a fish. And water can wick into the center of the fly line, which tends to drown the end. Some anglers prefer to use the Nail Knot to add a short, heavy length of monofilament to the line end. Then a loop is built in the other end of the monofilament strand. It makes more sense to me to install a permanent loop as in the next three methods.

The Whipped Loop has served me well for more than four decades. With a little practice it is possible to make a Whipped Loop in your fly line in less than two minutes. Loops have the advantage of not hanging up in the rod guides, and if constructed properly, all loops are stronger than the fly line. Loops allow a quick change of leaders to meet different fishing conditions. Loops also seal off the end so water doesn't wick into the line.

The Double Nail Knot Loop is another way of constructing a loop similar to the Whipped Loop. Instead of using whipped thread to secure the loop, two Nail Knots of 10- or 12-pound-test monofilament are used and then coated with a flexible cement such as Pliobond to form a smooth connection.

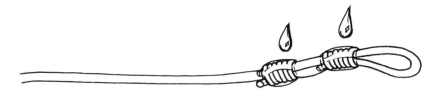

The Braided Line Loop is perhaps the best way to build loops in both ends of your fly line. It is very flexible and rides smoothly through the guides. With larger lines such as 9- to 14-weight, the Braided Line Loop is the strongest loop. The Whipped Loop and Double Nail Knot Loop can be severed by the leader under pressure from a very strong fish, and the game is lost.

CONNECTING THE TIPPET WITH A HEMOSTAT

Connecting a fragile tippet to the leader can be frustrating and time consuming. Dr. Mark Lamos has a quick method that delivers a connection stronger than a Blood Knot or Surgeon's Knot. With practice, you'll be able to make this connection in less than a minute.

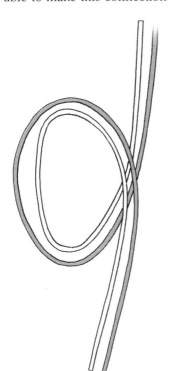

Step 1: Place the tippet and leader alongside of and opposite each other. Make sure the tippet is to the right. Form a loop. Pinch and hold the leader and tippet firmly at the top of the loop.

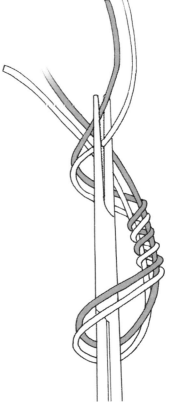

Step 2: Continue to pinch and hold the leader and tippet firmly at the top of the loop. Insert the hemostat into the loop and make three twists of the loop. Then gently grasp the leader end and the tippet and withdraw them through the loop.

Step 3: Remove the hemostat and tease all four strands to carefully and firmly close the knot.

Step 4: When the knot is completely closed, trim the ends.

Note: Using a hemostat is recommended when connecting lines no larger than 10-pound-test. With heavier lines, the fingers often perform better. Instead of using the hemostat in step 2, insert your first finger into the loop and make three twists. Now insert your thumb into the loop, and with your thumb and finger, grasp the two lines to the right and tease them through. Once through, moisten the knots and make sure to pull all four strands tight before trimming the ends.

SPEEDY NAIL KNOT

The Speedy Nail Knot is used to attach the butt section of a leader to a fly line. With practice, the Speedy Nail Knot can be attached to the fly line in a few seconds. Since all of the leader used to build a Speedy Knot must be drawn through the formed coils, the leader or butt section must be knot-free.

The Speedy Nail Knot can only be attached to the fly line end. If a Nail Knot is secured anywhere else on a fly line, the Tube Nail Knot is needed. While the drawing looks complicated, the Speedy Nail Knot is not difficult to tie if you follow the steps.

You need a needle to tie this knot. The smallest possible needle should be used. The needle supports the lines so they don't flop around while you are building the knot. The advantage of using the thinnest needle is that a thin needle leaves little space to be tightened once the Nail Knot is formed and the needle is extracted from under the coils. When a tube is used to form a Nail Knot, considerable teasing and tightening of the coils is required after the tube is removed.

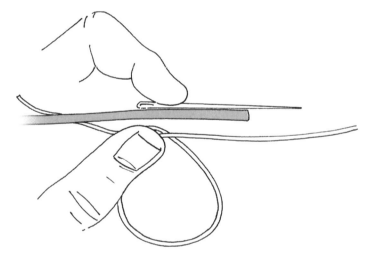

Step 1: Pinch together a needle, the fly line end, and the butt section of the leader with the needle on top, the fly line in the middle, and the leader butt below. The leader end should extend about an inch beyond the other two. You will need to grip this end to close the knot. Grasp the other end of the butt section or a knot-free leader and

make a loop. A common mistake is to form a loop with the leader hanging just below the fly line and needle. You must form the loop with the other end of the butt section or knot-free leader so that a long loop results.

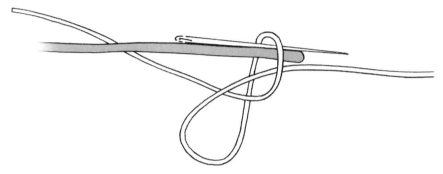

Step 2: While pinching the fly line, the needle, and the two ends of the leader with your left hand, grasp the right side of the loop with your right hand below the line and needle and make a complete turn around the fly line, the needle, and two strands of leader. It is important to grasp the right side of the leader no more than 2 inches from the fly line and needle and keep tension on the leader. If you grasp it too far away and any slack occurs, the coils tend to spring into a mess when winding. Begin making turns of the leader toward the hand holding the needle, leader, and line.

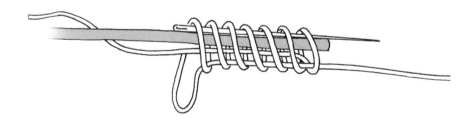

Step 3: Make five to seven complete turns around the fly line, the needle, and two strands of leader. Attempt to keep the coils close together as they will look when the knot is finished. This makes it easier to finally close the knot.

Step 4: The closer together the coils are at this stage the easier the knot will be to close properly. After making five to seven coils, tease the coils so they lie together and gently pull on the forward end of the leader until all slack in the loop has passed under the coils and the Nail Knot forms on the fly line. Remove the needle.

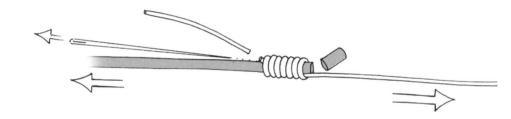

Step 5: Grasp the tag end and pull on the main leader section to close the Nail Knot. If you pull on the main leader and are not holding onto the short end, all the coils will slip off the line. Firmly pull the two lines ends to close the Speedy Nail Knot. Then trim the tag end flush with the coils.

CONNECTING OR REPAIRING FLY LINES

If a fly line is damaged or cut, it's easy to repair the sections. Also, some anglers do not like to loop shooting tapers or heads to the shooting line. They prefer a smooth connection. With a short section of 50-pound-test hollow braided monofilament, the chore is easy. Two popular hollow braided lines are Cortland braided mono running line and Gudebrod 50-pound butt leader. For fly lines 6 or smaller, I recommend using 30-pound-test hollow braided monofilament.

Cut a section of braided hollow line about 8 inches long. Tease open the end of the braided line with a small finishing nail or back of a large needle to allow the fly line access. Insert one fly line end approximately 4 inches into the core of the braided line. Insert the other fly line end in the opposite end of the braided line until the two fly lines touch. Make a 10- or 12-turn Nail Knot using 10- or 12-pound-test monofilament to secure both ends of the braided line, and coat the Nail Knots with Pliobond or a similar flexible glue. Coat only the Nail Knots so the rest of the hollow braided line can grip like a Chinese finger.

5

Wire Knots

NON-SLIP LOOP IN NICKEL-TITANIUM WIRE

Compared to the older plastic-coated braided wire, nickel-titanium wire is very flexible, thin, and strong. It is plastic-coated and some manufacturers suggest that monofilament knots can be used with it. But serious fishermen have discovered that most monofilament knots will fail under the stress of fighting a strong fish.

A knot that has performed exceedingly well with this type of wire is the Non-Slip Loop.

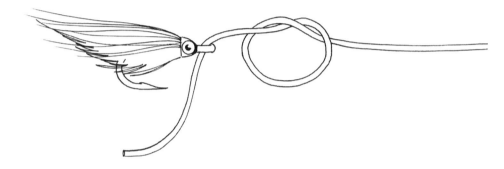

Step 1: Make an Overhand Knot and insert the tag end of the wire through the eye of the hook or swivel.

Step 2: Pass the tag end back through the Overhand Knot.

Step 3: Make two or three turns with the tag end around the main line. Adjust the loop size. (For information on how to do this, see the Non-Slip Loop in chapter 7.)

Step 4: Pull on the tag end to close the knot. Then trim the tag end.

FIGURE-8 KNOT

The Figure-8 Knot is very safe when used with the older type of braided wire. It is not as strong when used with the more modern nickel-titanium wire. It may look too simple to be effective, but it is a good knot when used with braided wire from 10- to 60-pound-test. The Figure-8 Knot is not recommended in anything but braided wire.

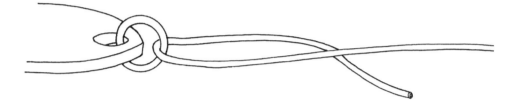

Step 1: Insert the tag end about 3 inches through the hook eye and carry the tag end under the main line.

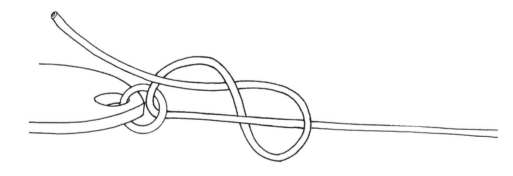

Step 2: Bring the tag end over the main line and back through the loop in front of the hook eye.

FIGURE-8 KNOT ▨ 69

Step 3: This is the critical part of forming the Figure-8 Knot. Gently grasp the main line but tighten the knot by pulling all slack from the knot with only the tag end. Any slack drawn through the knot by the main line will put kinked wire in front of the hook eye and spoil the action of the fly or lure.

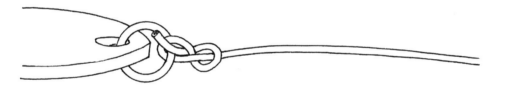

Step 4: Trim the tag end.

HAYWIRE TWIST

Solid trolling wire requires a special knot called the Haywire Twist. It can be used to attach a hook or swivel to wire line and sometimes to make a wire loop. When securing an Albright Knot with monofilament to solid wire, first make a loop and flatten the loop slightly. Then build the Albright inside the loop. Without a loop, the Albright Knot may slither through when you are fighting a strong fish.

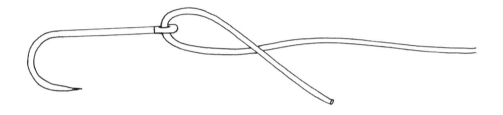

Step 1: Insert the tag end through the hook eye and cross the tag end over the main line, making an X with the wire. Pinch the wire at the X and form the desired size loop.

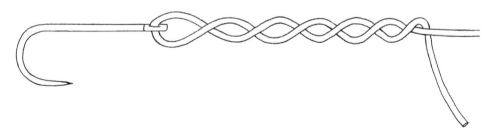

Step 2: Firmly hold the X you created and make a half turn twist, forming a tight X in the wire. Both the tag end and the main line must be held so that an X is formed each time a half turn is made.

Caution: You must form an X each time and turn and tighten it. If the tag end is simply wound around the main line, the knot may fail. Make 3 1/2 Xs and the main line will lie straight.

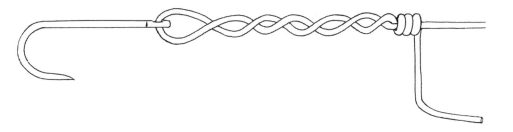

Step 3: Make 3 or 4 circular wraps with the tag end around the main line. Be sure to place each wrap snugly against the preceding one. Form a right angle "handle" with the tag end. Work the handle back and forth; if the circular wraps are close together, the wire will eventually break, leaving a smooth edge.

Important: Never cut the tag end because doing so will leave a sharp cutting end.

Step 4: A finished knot looks like this.

TIP

Solid trolling wire can be difficult to hold while you are making a Haywire Twist. Fold the wire around a large hook shank and use the hook to stabilize the wire while you build the knot.

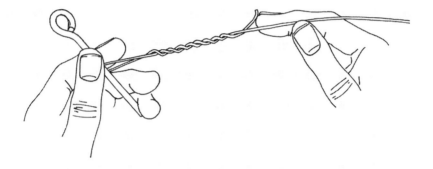

6

Finishing

WHIP FINISH

The Whip Finish is a useful knot for many situations. Illustrated here is a finished knot made for securing a fly that is being tied. A Whip Finish can also be used to secure a whipped loop in a fly line, as well as for other purposes. Some fly tiers think it is difficult to tie, but once you have learned it, you will rarely use a mechanical device to finish your flies.

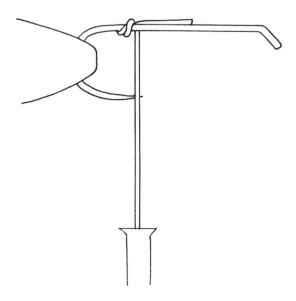

Step 1: To secure line to the hook, lay it along the hook shank and make two wraps over the hook and thread away from the tag end. Hold the bobbin with your left hand and form the Whip Finish with your right hand.

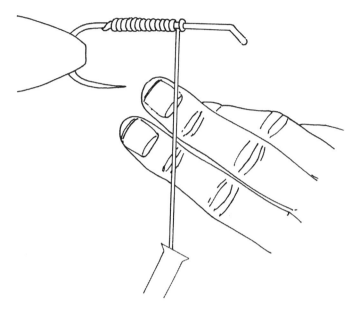

Step 2: Wrap the line around the hook a number of times. Secure the wraps in the hook and, keeping the line tight, place your first two fingers behind the line and under the hook.

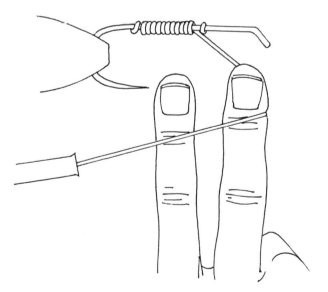

Step 3: Position your middle finger against the line and spread your fingers apart.

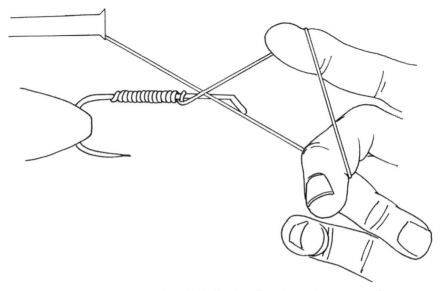

Step 4: Twist your hand clockwise, forming a loop around both fingers. Move the loop to the far side of the hook by keeping your index finger above the hook and your middle finger below the hook. It is important that the lower part of the loop always passes underneath the hook and that the top of the loop passes above the hook.

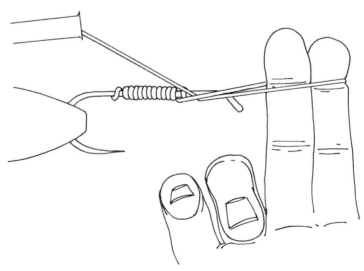

Step 5: Keep the loop beyond the hook under tension and bring your two fingers together so they touch.

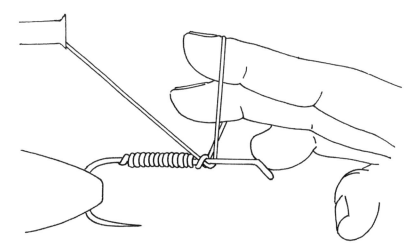

Step 6: Keep the loop above and behind the hook and your fingers together. Then twist your hand so that it is above and parallel to the hook.

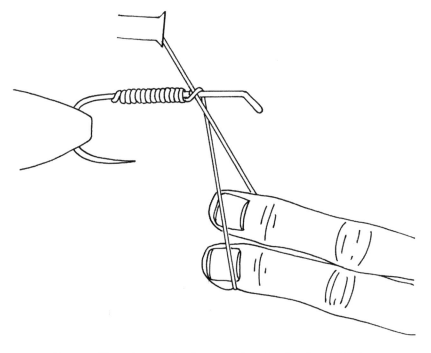

Step 7: Now lower the loop under the hook and bring your hand in front of the hook.

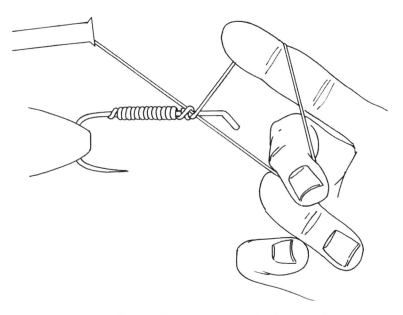

Step 8: Spread your fingers to open the loop and move the loop beyond the hook, keeping your upper finger above the hook and your lower finger below the hook. Repeat steps 2 through 6 until the desired number of turns (3-10) is placed on the hook.

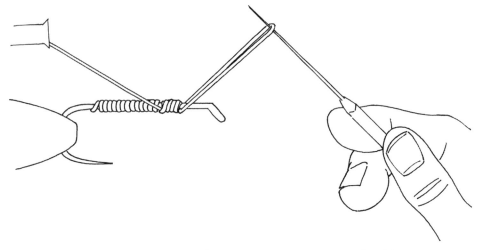

Step 9: To ensure perfect closure, insert a smooth, thin object inside the loop and draw on the bobbin end of the line.

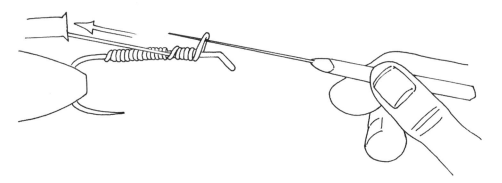

Step 10: Continue to draw on the line until the loop is nearly closed. Remove the object holding the loop and firmly tighten it. Trim the end flush.

TIP

Over time, nylon lines will deteriorate if they are exposed to sunlight, fluorescent light, or dry conditions. You should replace ultra-thin "X" size trout tippet spools every two years if you carry them in your fly vest. Make sure to label your nylon spools so you can keep track of how old they are.

ALTERNATE WHIP FINISH

This is another method of making a Whip Finish. It is often used to secure a rope end requiring a series of wraps. In this example we are securing the thread used to wrap a rod guide.

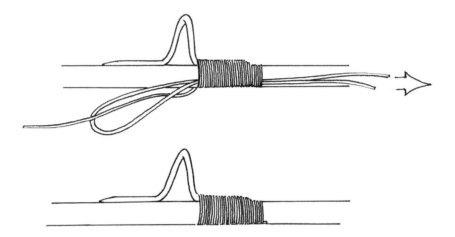

Step 1: After wrapping a foot on a rod guide with thread, secure the wraps with this Alternate Whip Finish to make sure they won't come loose. Before making the final eight or ten wraps, lay the two legs of a loop of 4- to 6-pound-test monofilament alongside the foot of the rod guide. Continue to make the final eight to ten wraps around both the guide foot and the two legs of the mono loop with light pressure. When enough wraps have been made, clip the thread to leave about 4 inches, being sure to keep tension on the thread end. If you fail to maintain tension on the thread end, all wraps will unravel. Insert the thread end through the mono loop, continuing to keep tension on the thread end.

Step 2: Grip the two legs of the monofilament loop and pull the thread end under and out from the wraps while keeping tension on the thread. Clip the thread and coat the wraps with Pliobond or some other flexible glue.

7

Loops

There are a number of situations where you'll need to join two lines together with loops. You may need to join the fly line backing to the rear of the fly line or connect the leader to the front of the line. Loops offer some flexibility if you need to switch lines. Perhaps you are fly fishing a short leader in fast water. Then you move to a long, calm flat pool where you need a longer leader to make the best presentation. If you have a loop in the fly line end, substituting another leader is an easy matter.

Loop knots where the tag end projects toward the fly and not toward the rod are less likely to snag on vegetation. To easily make a loop of any size, use a Non-Slip Loop or a Kreh Loop.

SIX-TURN SURGEON'S LOOP

The Six-Turn Surgeon's Loop is quick and easy to tie and will usually test close to 100 percent of line strength. Some anglers use it instead of the Bimini Twist. The loop works well in monofilament, fluorocarbon, Dacron, and braided gel-spun lines. With gel-spun, place a drop of Loctite 406 glue on the knot to ensure the knot will hold.

Step 1: Fold the tag end over the line to form a loop.

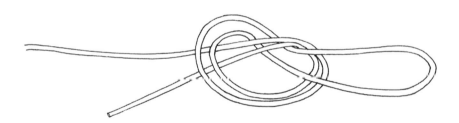

Step 2: Make an Overhand Knot with the loop end.

Step 3: Repeat this five times (making a six-turn Over-hand Knot, or Triple Surgeon's Knot). Try to pinch each turn close to the last one. This aids in a better closure.

Step 4: Insert the fingers of one hand into the loop end. Grasp the tag end and main line with your other hand and slowly draw the knot closed. It is important that your fingers are inside the loop so you can exert equal pressure on both legs as you close the knot. Be sure that none of the turns overlap or the knot will be weak. Once the knot is closed, keep your fingers inside the loop and pull firmly on the main line and then on the tag end to close tightly. Trim the tag end.

TIP

One drop of Loctite 406 worked with a needle into a braided knot (gel-spun or Dacron) will usually make the knot as strong as the line with no knot in it.

CONNECTING LOOP-TO-LOOPS

Unless properly connected, loop-to-loop knots lose much of their strength. An improper connection is a girth hitch that tends to cut the line under stress. To properly connect any loop-to-loop connection before closing it, form a square knot.

It is important to realize that gel-spun lines tied with the conventional square knot connection will often disengage during the battle and the knot will fail. For a reliable connection, be sure to follow the instructions in step 3.

This is a girth hitch, a weak connection.

Before closing the loop-to-loop, form a square knot to connect all lines except for braided gel-spun lines.

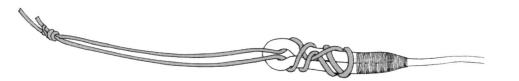

When fighting fish with gel-spun and other modern braided lines, a different connection is required. To form a secure loop-to-loop connection, insert the braided loop through the fly line loop. Then make a half twist with the gel-spun and again slip this through the fly line loop. Repeat this at least one or two more times. Tease the twists created so that they do not overlap as they are drawn closed. When properly closed, the connection resembles a braid.

TIP

What breaks most knots is a jerk on the line, so you should test lines with a jerk. Determining whether one knot is superior to another is simple. Take two hooks from the same box and tie a knot in each hook. Grasp the two hooks with pliers, and with your other hand, jerk the two lines until one breaks. Repeat this test ten times, and you will know which knot is stronger.

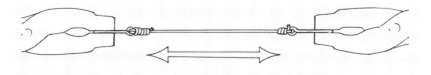

WHIPPING A LOOP

Many fly fishermen prefer a loop in the fly line end. It permits a quick change of leaders and is an easy way to replace a fly line. It also stops water from seeping into the fly line end and causing the line to sink. Because loops are rounded, they almost never catch in the guides when you're fighting a fish. The two most popular line loops are the Whipped Loop and the Braided Loop.

To make a Whipped Loop, you will need a fly-tying bobbin equipped with strong thread such as size A nylon or Kevlar, a razorblade, and flexible glue, such as Pliobond. With practice, you should be able to build this loop in two or three minutes. Properly made, a Whipped Loop is stronger than the fly line.

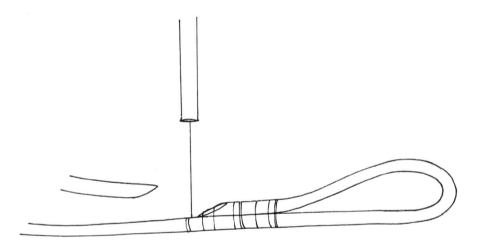

Step 1: Pull about 12 inches of thread off the bobbin. Remove the spool from the base of the bobbin and wrap the thread five times around one leg of the bobbin; then reinstall the spool. The five wraps allow you to swing the bobbin under tension. If additional thread is needed, you will have to turn the spool to obtain it. With a razorblade, make a slanted cut in the fly line end (do not remove the finish from the fly line). Fold the end against the main line to form a loop about ³/₄ inch long. Wrap the end of the thread four times over these two lines.

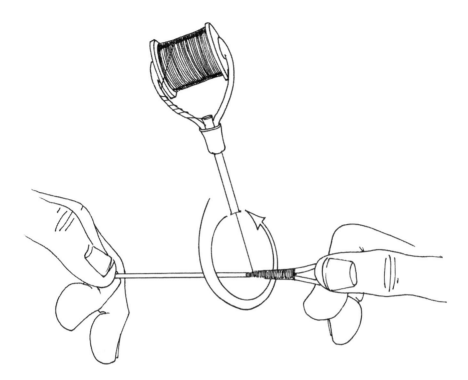

Step 2: Pinch the wraps and the loop and begin to swing the bobbin, making more wraps around the fly line. The harder you swing the bobbin, the tighter the coils and the stronger the connection will be. Swing it too hard and you might break the thread and have to start over. Make enough wraps to pass beyond the tapered end and then return over the doubled ends.

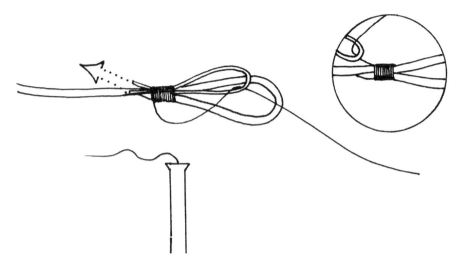

Step 3: To secure the wraps, use the fly tier's Whip Finish. If you don't know the Whip Finish, cut an 8- or 10-inch length of 4- or 6-pound-test monofilament and form a horseshoe shape with it. (See Alternate Whip Finish.)

Step 4: Lay the two legs of the monofilament on the wraps and pinch them to keep them in position. *Gently* swing the bobbin eight to ten times around the two legs of the monofilament. Continue to pinch wraps and thread and clip about 6 inches of the thread emitting from the bobbin.

Step 5: Slip the thread end into the U of the monofilament and then pull on the two monofilament legs. This will draw the thread end under the gentle wraps, forming a Whip Finish.

To be sure the loop will be strong, insert a nail or a similar thin rod into the loop. Grasp the nail in one hand and with your other hand, firmly grip the fly line and try to pull the loop apart. If the loop slips or unravels, you did not swing the bobbin hard enough.

Step 6: Coat the wraps with Pliobond or another flexible glue.

BRAIDED FLY LINE LOOP

Many experienced fishermen prefer the Braided Line Loop method of attaching a loop to a fly line or a shooting head. The braided line acts like a Chinese finger; the harder a fish pulls on the fly, the tighter the braid grips the fly line. The Braided Loop has several advantages: it's extremely strong, very flexible, and offers a smooth connection that doesn't catch as it flows through the rod guides.

Size is important when building a Braided Line Loop. For connecting a leader to the loop or a shooting head to a shooting line, a loop no longer than one inch is recommended. The loop attached to the rear of the fly line should be at least 8–10 inches long, making it easy to loop the fly line on and off the backing.

For most fly line connections, 50-pound braided monofilament is best. For smaller fly line, use 30-pound-test braided mono. Many fishermen prefer the 50-pound Gudebrod Butt Leader, which has a tighter braid and is not waxed. Other anglers prefer Cortland's Braided Mono Running Line. Either one works.

To make a Braided Fly Line Loop, you need a few tools. A splicing needle will be used to draw the braid through the inner core. You'll also need a large sewing needle and a small finishing nail or fly-tying bodkin to aid in opening the braid. Twelve inches of braided mono is enough to connect to a fly leader or shooting head. To make a larger loop in the rear of the fly line, begin with about 30 inches of braided mono.

Step 1: To make a splicing needle, you need a 26-inch piece of very fine wire; the finest guitar string or size 2, 3, or 4 trolling wire will work. Bend the wire into a U, making sure the end of the bend is compressed tightly. Connect the two ends using a Haywire Twist to something you can grasp—a large split ring is ideal. (You'll find one at any key shop.)

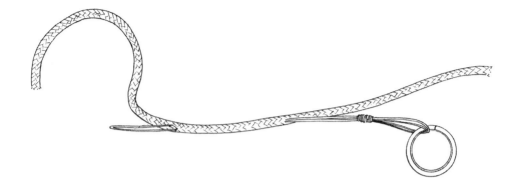

Step 2: Insert the splicing needle into the braided mono about 2 inches from the end. If you have difficulty getting the wire inside the braid, tease an opening by inserting the large needle or bodkin. Push the splicing needle through the core of the braid.

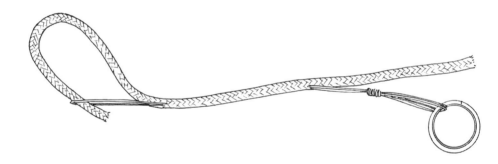

Step 3: Force the end of the splicing needle outside the braid and trap the other end of the mono in the eye of the needle.

Step 4: Pull the end of the mono trapped in the eye of the needle inside the braid and continue pulling until the end exits the braid. Grasp the braided mono end and pull it through the core of the braided mono until you create a loop of the desired size.

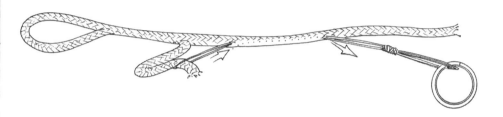

Step 5: Reinsert the splicing needle about 2 inches below where the tag end exited the braided mono. Trap the tag end in the eye of the splicing needle and pull it again through the hollow braid, causing the end to exit the braid.

Step 6: Tease the braid a   and clip off the tag end. By strokin   e tag end will disappear inside the

Step 7: Insert the fly line in the hollow core and tease it forward in the core until it is about ⅛ inch past the buried tag end.

Step 8: It is important to secure the braided mono where the fly line entered it at the rear. Do this with a ten- to twelve-turn Nail Knot using 10- or 12-pound-test monofilament. Firmly close the Nail Knot and coat it with Pliobond or a similar flexible glue.

NON-SLIP LOOP

A loop knot is one of the most useful knots in fishing. A loop in the line allows the lure or fly to be more active during the retrieve. Anglers have used loops in monofilament and wire for decades, but most loop knots have some disadvantages. First, the tag end of most loop knots protrudes either outward or forward. This stub, even if very short, will tangle a thick tippet and often catch grass in the water, spoiling the retrieve. Second, most loop knots are not as strong as the line they are tied with and cannot be adjusted to loop size. Finally, many loop knots can be tied only in fluorocarbon or monofilament and not in braided wire.

The Non-Slip Loop overcomes most of these disadvantages. It doesn't snag. The tag end protrudes toward the fly, lure, or hook, reducing the chance of snagging grass during the retrieve. It is strong. When tied correctly, it will test near or at full-line strength in all kinds of weights—150-pound-test monofilament or 8X tippet. It is versatile. You can use it to make a simple loop or a loop to attach the lure, fly, or bare hook. You can build the loop to any desired size. And best of all, it is perhaps the most effective knot for tying a loop in braided wire, especially the modern multi-strand wire.

The knot may appear to be difficult to tie, but it is rather easy. You make an Overhand Knot, insert the tag end through the hook eye, bring the tag end back through the Overhand Knot, and make a number of turns with the tag end before inserting the tag end a final time through the Overhand Knot. Now let's do it step-by-step.

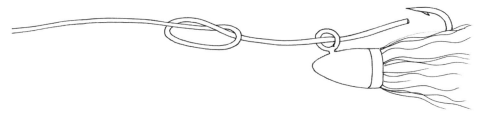

Step 1: To attach a hook, lure, or fly, make an Overhand Knot in the line before you insert it through the hook eye.

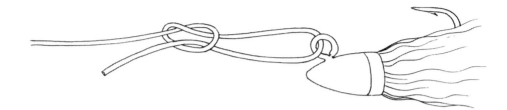

Step 2: Pass the tag end back through the Overhand Knot the same way it came out of the knot.

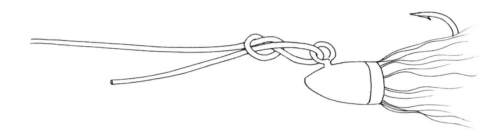

Step 3: Large loops can cause problems, so it is best to make smaller loops. You can adjust the size of the loop as follows. After making step 2, use your thumb and forefinger to pinch together the Overhand Loop and the line passing through it. By drawing on the main line, you can then reduce the Overhand Loop. Continue pinching the two lines and pull on the tag end. This action moves the now-smaller Overhand Knot down until it touches the hook eye, further reducing the loop's size.

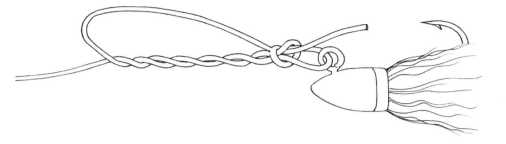

Step 4: Start making turns with the tag end around the main line. It is the number of turns that determines the knot's strength. For lines testing 8X to 6-pound-test, make seven turns; for 8- to 12-pound-test, make five turns; for 15- to 40-pound-test, four turns; and for line heavier than that, make only two turns. For thin, flexible modern multi-strand plastic-coated braided wire lines, make three turns. For the older plastic-coated braided wire, two turns are enough.

The key to tying a strong Non-Slip Loop is to make the required turns with the tag end around the main line before you finish the knot.

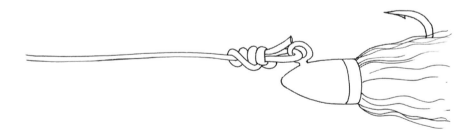

Step 5: To ensure maximum strength, pull on the main line, the tag end, and the lure or hook to firmly close the knot.

KREH LOOP

The Kreh Loop (named by others, not me) is slightly stronger than the Non-Slip Loop. The only difference between the Non-Slip Loop and the Kreh Loop is the way the tag end finishes the knot. The tag end of the Non-Slip Loop is inserted in the center of the Overhand Knot, while the Kreh Loop's tag end is passed through one side of the Overhand Knot and not through the center.

When correctly tied, the Kreh Loop is about 100 percent, even in a fragile 7X tippet. But since there's a loop in this knot, if the knot is used with a size 18 nymph, the knot will be larger than the fly. For freshwater trout I use the Kreh Loop or Non-Slip Loop only with hooks larger than size 12.

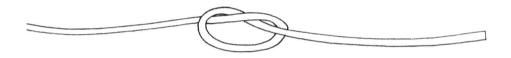

Step 1: Make an Overhand Knot in the line with the tag end. Allow about 4 to 5 inches of the tag end to extend through the knot to give you enough line to complete the knot.

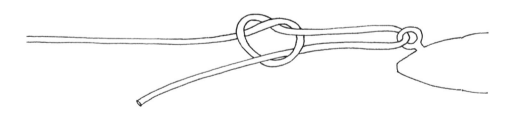

Step 2: Insert the tag end through the hook eye on the same side the tag end entered the Overhand Knot.

Step 3: Most of the time a small loop is desired. To adjust the loop size, pinch together the Overhand Knot and the point where the tag end returned through it. While pinching, gently pull on the main line. This will reduce the size of the Overhand Knot. Now gently pull on the tag end while continuing to pinch the lines. This will move the smaller Overhand Knot toward the hook eye, allowing you to control the loop size.

Step 4: Make the correct number of turns with the tag end around the main line. It is the number of turns that determines the knot's strength. For lines testing from 8X to 6-pound-test, make seven turns; for 8- to 12-pound-test, make five turns; for 15- to 40-pound-test, make four turns; for heavier line, make only two turns. For thinner, flexible modern multi-strand plastic-coated wire line, make three turns. For the older style thicker plastic-coated braided wire, two turns are enough.

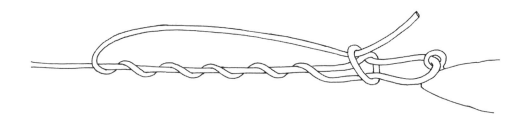

Step 5: After making the required turns with the tag end around the main line, pass the tag end through the side of the Overhand Knot (not through the center).

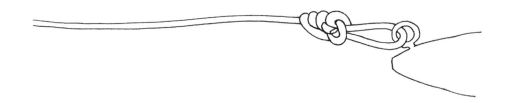

Step 6: To properly close the knot, pull on the tag end, the main line, and the hook. Hint: If it appears that the loop may be a little too large, pull harder on the tag end to decrease the loop size. If the loop seems too small, pull harder on the main line when closing. Trim the tag end.

SURGEON'S LOOP

The Surgeon's Loop is the easiest loop to tie and is used often. It is not as strong as the Non-Slip Loop or the Kreh Loop. It can be tied in both monofilament and fluorocarbon but is not recommended in any braided line. It is necessary to pull on all four strands (two forming the loop) and the tag end and the main line to obtain maximum strength. To close the Surgeon's Loop properly after it is formed, insert a smooth object (such as a hemostat) in the loop to ensure equal tension is applied to both strands. With lines testing less than 10 pounds, you can make a stronger knot if you pass the doubled line through the Overhand Knot three times instead of two.

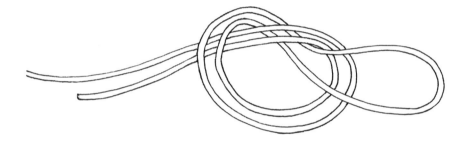

Step 1: Double the line and form an Overhand Knot.

Step 2: Pass the loop end through the Overhand a second time (if line tests less than 10 pounds, pass the loop end through the Overhand a third time).

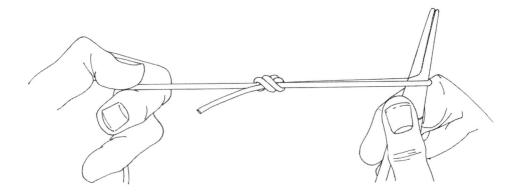

Step 3: Insert a smooth object such as a hemostat in the loop end and apply firm pressure on the main line, then on the tag end to ensure all four strands are tightly closed.

TIP

Store quarter-pound spools of monofilament in Koozie holders. Insert the spool into the Koozie and trim it with a sharp knife, so the Koozie is flush with the top of the inserted spool. Leave the line end outside so you can easily pull what's needed.

8

Attaching Hooks, Swivels, and Flies

WHY A CLINCH KNOT IS DIFFICULT TO CLOSE

The Clinch Knot is a popular knot, and there are a good number of variations. The Improved Clinch Knot, Blood Knot, and Uni-Knot are all forms of the Clinch Knot. Fishermen frequently have trouble closing a clinch-type knot. If the knot is not properly closed, it won't be as strong as it needs to be. The problem with closing is easy to fix.

Closing a Clinch Knot

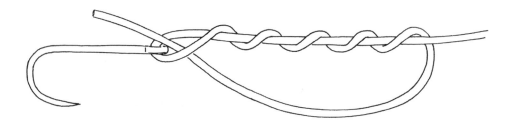

Step 1: Form the Improved Clinch Knot. After the Clinch Knot is formed, the tag end often leaves a gap.

Step 2: To firmly close the Clinch Knot, remove the gap by pulling on the tag end so that all loose line can be securely closed.

Closing a Blood Knot

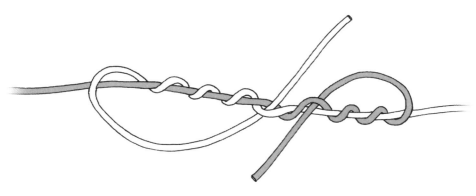

Step 1: Form the Blood Knot. Pull on the tag ends to eliminate the gaps.

Step 2: With the gaps gone, the short tag ends lie against the main line.

Step 3: Pull the tag ends tight and then trim them close.

DOUBLED CLINCH KNOT

Properly tied and closed, the Doubled Clinch Knot tests at least 80 percent line strength. This connection performs well even with heavier monofilament and fluorocarbon but is not recommended when joining to braided gel-spun or Dacron lines.

The Doubled Clinch Knot is useful for spin casters and plug casters, who often spool their reels with light lines to gain distance when casting light lures. They want to add a heavier length between the light line and the lure. This knot creates a small connection that flows through the rod guides easily and works well for this purpose.

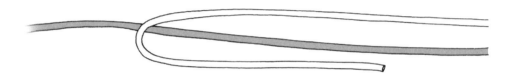

Step 1: Make a U in the portion of line to be attached to the hook. Place the thinner line behind the U.

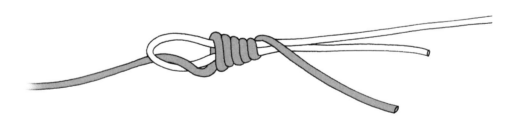

Step 2: Make five complete turns with the tag end of the thinner line around the U. Try to keep all wraps as close together as possible.

Step 3: Now make four complete turns back toward the bend in the U, trying to keep all coils as close as possible. Insert the tag end through the thinner line loop.

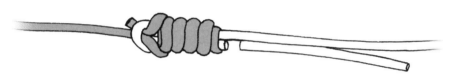

Step 4: Carefully tease all coils together toward the bend in the U. Always pull on the tag end first while firmly holding the two ends of the U and then pull firmly on the main line. You may have to repeat this several times to properly close the knot. After closing the knot, clip the tag ends.

FISHERMAN'S KNOT

This knot has been renamed several times. In March of 1979, Dupont published a drawing of this knot that was called the Heiliger's Knot. It also has been referred to as the 16-20, the Pitzen, and other names. When I first encountered it many years ago, it was called a Fisherman's Knot, so that's the name I use for it. The Fisherman's Knot is a quick and easy knot to tie, and it performs well. With lines testing more than 15 pounds, it will out-perform the Improved Clinch Knot. With lines testing more than 20-pound-test, the Improved Clinch Knot is difficult to close well with bare hands.

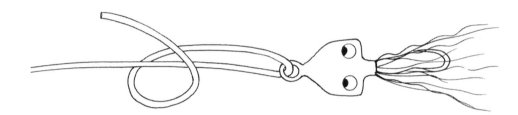

Step 1: Insert the tag end of the line through the hook eye, fold the tag end back under the main line, and begin making coils around the doubled line.

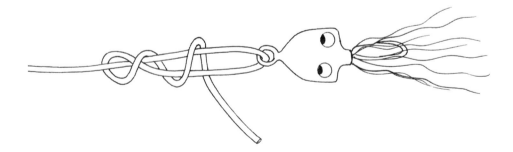

Step 2: With lines testing more than 20 pounds, make three complete coils around the doubled line. With weaker lines, make five coils.

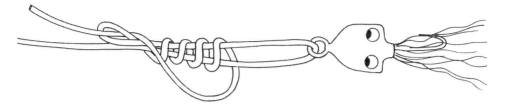

Step 3: After making the desired number of coils, take the tag end back toward the main line and put the tag end through the loop.

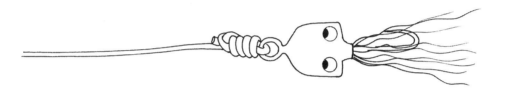

Step 4: Moisten the coils and lightly push coils together. Then pull firmly on the main line to properly seat the knot. Trim the tag end.

TRILENE KNOT

The Trilene Knot is one of the strongest knots for connecting monofilament or fluorocarbon lines to hooks. It is not recommended for braided gel-spun lines. The Trilene Knot is difficult to close properly by hand with lines testing more than 20 pounds. Because the line must be passed through the hook eye twice, this knot cannot be used with hooks that have small eyes.

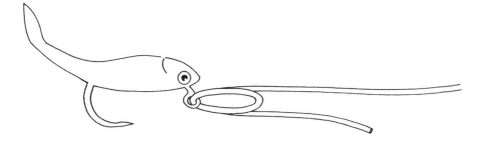

Step 1: Pass the tag end of the line through the eye hook twice and form two small loops of approximately the same size in front of the eye hook.

Step 2: Make five complete turns around the main line with the tag end. Then pass the tag end through both loops.

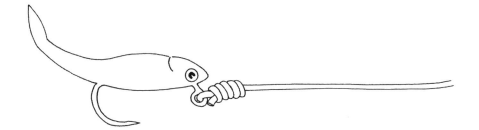

Step 3: Lubricate the knot with water or saliva and firmly pull on the hook, tag end, and the main line to properly seat the knot. Trim the tag end.

TIP

Spare spools of spinning reel line can be easily nicked and damaged. Placing a spool in an old, heavy sock is an easy way to protect it when it is being stored in a tackle box.

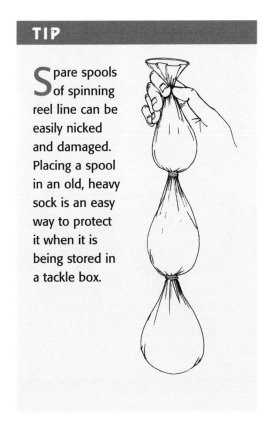

PALOMAR KNOT

The Palomar Knot is one of the strongest knots, and it performs well in all types of fishing lines. It has the highest strength of any of the knots I tested for use with braided gel-spun lines. It is quick to learn and easy to tie. But the Palomar has two disadvantages: First, the eye of the swivel or hook has to be large enough to allow the doubled line to be drawn through. Second, once the double line passes through the eye of the hook, swivel, lure, or fly, it has to be inserted through the loop. This is often bothersome with larger lures, especially those that have multiple treble hooks.

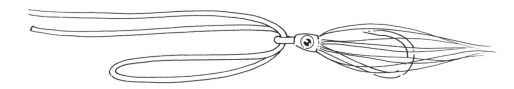

Step 1: Double the line by folding the tag end over the main line. Pass the loop end of the doubled line through the hook eye.

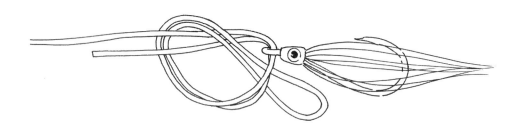

Step 2: Form an Overhand Knot in the standing part of the doubled line with the loop end.

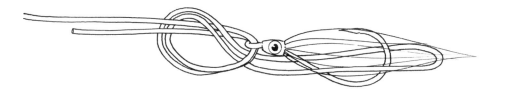

Step 3: Pass the fly, lure, hook, or swivel through the Overhand Knot.

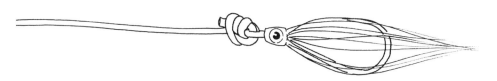

Step 4: Pull on the main line to begin tightening the knot. Further tighten the knot by pulling on the tag end. Pull on both lines for final closure. Clip the tag end close to the hook eye.

TIP

Cutting Gel-Spun Braided Lines

Gel-spun braided lines are difficult to cut with normal clippers and scissors. I've found that Fiskars for Kids scissors do a great job. They cost about $3. You'll find other inexpensive tools designed specifically for fishing tasks at your local fishing shop.

ORVIS OR BECKER KNOT

Some years ago, the Orvis company conducted a search to locate a good knot for attaching the leader tippet to the fly. Larry Becker of Rockford, Illinois, came up with a variation of the Figure-8 Knot. I think it's the best knot to use if you want a strong knot for fragile tippets. Added advantages are that it's easy to tie and requires little tippet material. I encourage all trout fishermen to experiment with this knot.

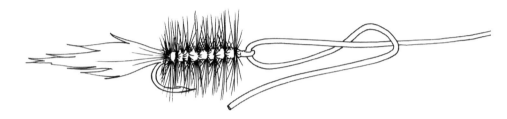

Step 1: Insert the tag end through hook eye and bring the tag end toward you. Take the tag end under the main line and then bring it over the main line as shown.

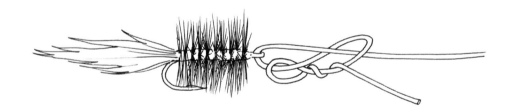

Step 2: Pass the tag end under and through the large loop immediately in front of the hook eye. Then make two wraps with the tag end around the line nearest you.

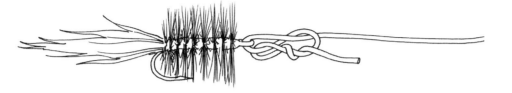

Step 3: Wet the connection and, while holding the fly and tag end, nearly close the knot.

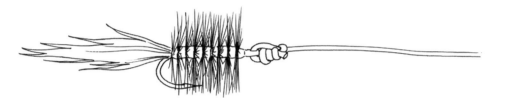

Step 4: Release the tag end and pull on the main line while holding the hook to firmly close. Trim the tag end.

SNELLING A HOOK

One of the oldest methods of attaching a line to a hook is snelling. The knot is actually a Nail Knot and is one of the strongest connections. Many tarpon fishermen prefer this knot because once the snell is in place the hook cannot twist when retrieved. The disadvantage of snelling a hook is that the shank must be bare where the coils are established.

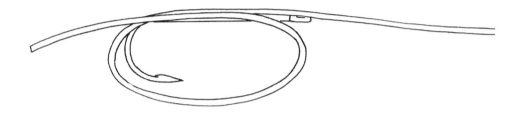

Step 1: Lay the main line parallel to and on top of the hook shank. If a turned-up or -down eye is used, you should insert the tag end through the hook eye so the hook runs straighter on the retrieve. Form a large loop with the tag end and lay it along the hook shank pointing toward the bend.

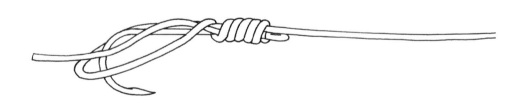

Step 2: Pinch both lines and the shank at the hook eye with your left hand and continue to firmly hold. With your right hand, grasp the loop and wrap it at least five times around the hook and both pieces of line lying against the shank near the hook eye. Make sure that the loop circles around the hook bend with each turn.

Step 3: Move the thumb and finger holding the line near the hook eye so they can trap the wraps made around the shank. Then pull on the main line to close the snell. Trim the stub extending from the snell and be sure you have closed the knot by firmly pulling on the main strand.

TIP

It's important to close a knot firmly. When attaching fragile trout tippets to small flies, such as size 16 or smaller, you'll find it is difficult to hold the fly when closing the knot. Place the hook on a foot of the stripping guide, hold one hand under the fly, and pull on the leader. If the knot should break during closure, the hand underneath will catch the fly.

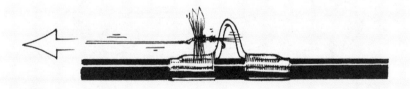

CAT'S PAW KNOT

The Cat's Paw Knot is versatile, and the two strands attaching it to a hook or swivel make it exceptionally strong. If one strand breaks during the battle, the fish remains connected to the angler with the other strand.

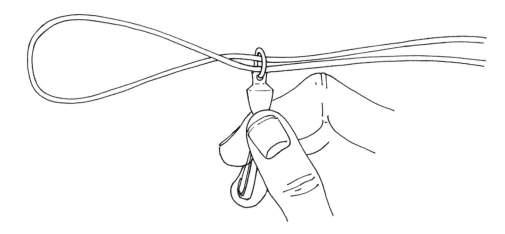

Step 1: First make a Bimini Twist or a Six-Turn Surgeon's Loop. Insert the loop of the knot through the ring of the swivel or the hook eye and make one twist.

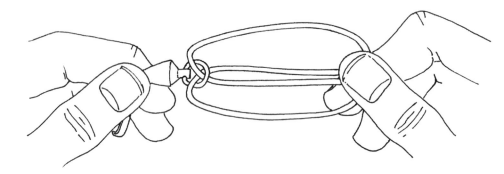

Step 2: Lay the loop end back against the standing lines, being careful to keep the one twist in the loop. Pinch the loop against the standing lines with your thumb and forefinger, forming a doubled loop.

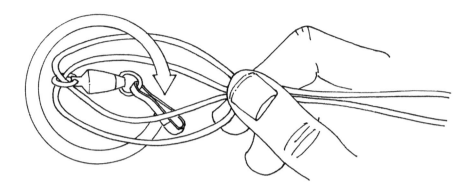

Step 3: Swing the hook or swivel through the doubled loop six times. Continue to hold the loop end and the standing part together so that the knot won't unravel.

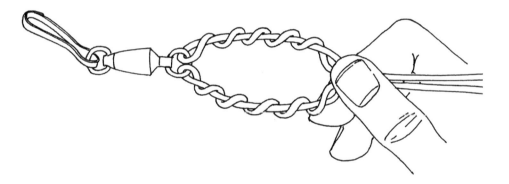

Step 4: After six passes through the doubled loop, the knot should look like this.

Step 5: Closing the knot will be a little difficult. Moisten the knot thoroughly. Hold the hook or swivel in one hand (use pliers if necessary) and both standing lines in the other. Pull on the hook or swivel to slide the knot down until all the twists seat firmly against the hook eye or swivel ring. You will probably need to alternate between pulling and pushing the twists together.

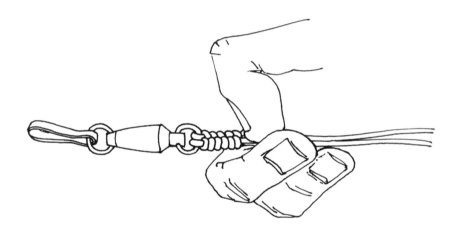

Step 6: When finished, the Cat's Paw Knot should resemble a pair of Clinch Knots.

HEMOSTAT QUICK CLINCH

One of the most frustrating things about trout fishing is trying to quickly tie on a tiny fly pattern, especially if your eyesight is not good, your fingers are cold and stiff, or the light is fading. The Hemostat Quick Clinch is not the strongest knot, but it is useful for tying flies on quickly. One of my friends, Dr. Mark Lamos, uses this knot successfully and lands some very large trout with it. It works well with monofilament and fluorocarbon line not heavier than 10-pound-test.

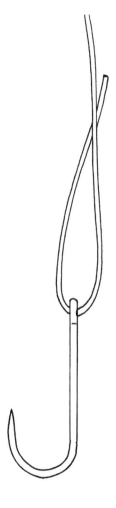

Step 1: Insert the tag end of the tippet through the hook eye to form the loop. If you have trouble doing this with tiny hooks, I suggest you purchase a special hook threader made by C&F Design, which is available from many fly shops. It's like the old-fashioned needle threader, and it works well.

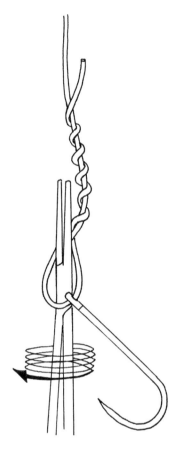

Step 2: Pinch the tag end and main line together and hold them firmly. Insert the hemostat into the loop and make six turns around the two lines with the tool. Be sure to insert the hemostat well into the loop so it does not slip out during twisting.

Step 3: While continuing to pinch the lines with one hand, use the other hand to grasp the very end of the tippet with the hemostat and lock the tool. (If you grasp only the end of the tag, you will use very little of the tippet to make the knot.) Pull the tag end through the loop and close the knot firmly.

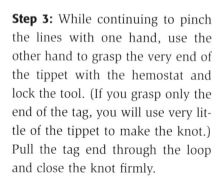

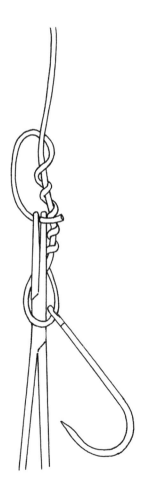

Step 4: To firmly secure the knot in small flies, grasp the hook bend and main line with the hemostat and pull. Clip the tag end.

Index of Knots